Linux Shell Scripting Bootcamp

The fastest way to learn Linux shell scripting

James Kent Lewis

BIRMINGHAM - MUMBAI

Linux Shell Scripting Bootcamp

First published: July 2017

Production reference: 1170717

Published by Packt Publishing Ltd.
Livery Place
35 Livery Street
Birmingham B3 2PB, UK.

ISBN 978-1-78728-110-3

www.packtpub.com

Credits

Author
James Kent Lewis

Reviewer
Thushara Jayawardena

Commissioning Editor
Pratik Shah

Acquisition Editor
Namrata Patil

Content Development Editor
Amrita Noronha

Technical Editor
Jovita Alva

Copy Editor
SAFIS
Laxmi Subramanian

Project Coordinator
Shweta H Birwatkar

Proofreader
SAFIS

Indexer
Pratik Shirodkar

Graphics
Tania Dutta

Production Coordinator
Arvindkumar Gupta

Cover Work
Arvindkumar Gupta

About the Author

James Kent Lewis has been in the computer industry for over 35 years. He started out writing basic programs in high school and used punch cards in college for his Pascal, Fortran, COBOL, and assembly language classes. Jim taught himself the C programming language by writing various utilities, including a fully-functional text editor, which he uses everyday.

He started out using DOS and AIX, and then OS/2. Linux is now his operating system of choice.

Jim has worked in the past for several companies, including IBM, Texas Instruments, Tandem, Raytheon, Hewlett-Packard, and others. Most of these positions dealt with low-level device drivers and operating system internals. In his spare time he likes to create video games in Java.

Jim has written articles for IBM Developer Works and has one patent. He has worked on Linux Utilities Cookbook with Packt Publishing.

Acknowledgement

First, I would like to thank Red Hat and CentOS for creating a great operating system. I used CentOS 6.8 exclusively in the writing of this book and it worked flawlessly. I would also like to thank my brother, David, for letting me bounce ideas off of him. Last, but certainly not least, I would like to thank my girlfriend, Gabriele. Her patience was greatly appreciated, and she also helped by letting me log into her Fedora laptop from time to time.

About the Reviewer

Thushara Jayawardena is a very strong asset in software development as well as in the software service industry with more than 15 years of experience in systems administrating. That experience has contributed to this book. The main responsibility of the current day job is performance engineering for a leading European ERP software provider. It translates to system configuration and installations, followed by end-to-end automated performance testing. Scripting is an integral part of all these components.

His spare time is spent partly developing a user guide for tourist attractions for Android and IOS devices. The cloud backend for the solution comprises Mongo Cloud DB services and Heroku app dynos, run on Nodejs. Thushara also spends time with systems on chip devices such as Raspberry Pi and Arduino-like boards. Here, the focus is on IOT-type solutions.

Thushara is a loving father and husband who values his family very much and makes sure homebrewing doesn't come between him and family. He's been living nomadic since 2007, or rather migrated to Sweden with his family and moved around a bit in Sweden, and currently is living south of the beautiful port city of Gothenburg. He enjoys Scandinavian life, simplicity, and respect very much and is keen on improving his skiing skills during the winters up in the Swedish mountains. He has also worked on Raspberry Pi Android Projects.

www.PacktPub.com

eBooks, discount offers, and more

Did you know that Packt offers eBook versions of every book published, with PDF and ePub files available? You can upgrade to the eBook version at www.PacktPub.com and as a print book customer, you are entitled to a discount on the eBook copy. Get in touch with us at customercare@packtpub.com for more details.

At www.PacktPub.com, you can also read a collection of free technical articles, sign up for a range of free newsletters and receive exclusive discounts and offers on Packt books and eBooks.

https://www.packtpub.com/mapt

Get the most in-demand software skills with Mapt. Mapt gives you full access to all Packt books and video courses, as well as industry-leading tools to help you plan your personal development and advance your career.

Why subscribe?

- Fully searchable across every book published by Packt
- Copy and paste, print, and bookmark content
- On demand and accessible via a web browser

Customer Feedback

Thanks for purchasing this Packt book. At Packt, quality is at the heart of our editorial process. To help us improve, please leave us an honest review on this book's Amazon page at www.amazon.com/dp/1787281108.

If you'd like to join our team of regular reviewers, you can e-mail us at customerreviews@packtpub.com. We award our regular reviewers with free eBooks and videos in exchange for their valuable feedback. Help us be relentless in improving our products!

Table of Contents

Preface

In Linux Shell Scripting Bootcamp, you will begin by learning the essentials of script creation. You will learn how to validate parameters and also how to check for the existence of files. Moving on, you will get well-versed with how variables work on a Linux system and how they relate to scripts. You'll also learn how to create and call subroutines and create interactive scripts. Finally, you will learn how to debug scripts and scripting best practices, which will enable you to write a great code every time! By the end of the book you will be able to write shell scripts that can dig data from the Web and process it efficiently.

What this book covers

Chapter 1, *Getting Started with Shell Scripting,* begins with the basics of script design. How to make a script executable is shown as is creating an informative `Usage` message. The importance of return codes is also covered with the use and validation of parameters.

Chapter 2, *Working with Variables*, discusses how to declare and use both environment and local variables. We also speak about how math is performed and how to work with arrays.

Chapter 3, *Using Loops and the sleep Command*, introduces the use of loops to perform iterative operations. It also shows how to create a delay in a script. The reader will also learn how to use loops and the `sleep` command in a script.

Chapter 4, *Creating and Calling Subroutines*, starts with some very simple scripts and then proceeds to cover some simple subroutines that take parameters.

Chapter 5, *Creating Interactive Scripts*, explains the use of the `read` built-in command to query the keyboard. Further, we explore some of the different options to read and also cover the use of traps.

Chapter 6, Automating Tasks with Scripts, describes the creation of scripts to automate a task. The proper way to use cron to run a script automatically at a specific time is covered. The archive commands `zip` and `tar` are also discussed for performing compressed backups.

Chapter 7, Working with Files, introduces the use of the redirection operator for writing out a file and use of `read` command for reading a file. Checksums and file encryption are also discussed, and a way to convert the contents of a file into a variable is also covered.

Chapter 8, Working with wget and curl, discusses the usage of `wget` and `curl` in scripts. Along with this, return codes are also discussed with a couple of example scripts.

Chapter 9, Debugging Scripts, explains some techniques to prevent common syntax and logic errors. A way to send output from a script to another terminal using the redirection operator was also discussed.

Chapter 10, Scripting Best Practices, discusses some practices and techniques that will help the reader create good code every time.

What you need for this book

Any Linux machine that has Bash should be able to run these scripts. This includes desktops, laptops, embedded devices, BeagleBone, and so on. Windows machines running Cygwin or some other emulated Linux environment will also work.

There are no minimum memory requirements.

Who this book is for

This book is for both GNU/Linux users who want to do amazing things with the shell and for advanced users looking for ways to make their lives with the shell more productive

Conventions

In this book, you will find a number of text styles that distinguish between different kinds of information. Here are some examples of these styles and an explanation of their meaning.

Code words in text, database table names, folder names, filenames, file extensions, pathnames, dummy URLs, user input, and Twitter handles are shown as follows: You can see that the `echo` statement `Start of x loop` was displayed A block of code is set as follows:

```
echo "Start of x loop"
x=0
while [ $x -lt 5 ]
do
 echo "x: $x"
 let x++
```

Any command-line input or output is written as follows:

```
guest1 $ ps auxw | grep script7
```

New terms and **important words** are shown in bold. Words that you see on the screen, for example, in menus or dialog boxes, appear in the text like this: "Clicking the **Next** button moves you to the next screen."

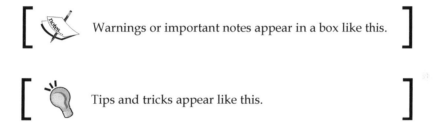

Warnings or important notes appear in a box like this.

Tips and tricks appear like this.

Reader feedback

Feedback from our readers is always welcome. Let us know what you think about this book—what you liked or disliked. Reader feedback is important for us as it helps us develop titles that you will really get the most out of.

To send us general feedback, simply e-mail feedback@packtpub.com, and mention the book's title in the subject of your message.

If there is a topic that you have expertise in and you are interested in either writing or contributing to a book, see our author guide at www.packtpub.com/authors.

Customer support

Now that you are the proud owner of a Packt book, we have a number of things to help you to get the most from your purchase.

Downloading the example code

You can download the example code files for this book from your account at http://www.packtpub.com. If you purchased this book elsewhere, you can visit http://www.packtpub.com/support and register to have the files e-mailed directly to you.

You can download the code files by following these steps:

1. Log in or register to our website using your e-mail address and password.
2. Hover the mouse pointer on the **SUPPORT** tab at the top.
3. Click on **Code Downloads & Errata**.
4. Enter the name of the book in the **Search** box.
5. Select the book for which you're looking to download the code files.
6. Choose from the drop-down menu where you purchased this book from.
7. Click on **Code Download**.

You can also download the code files by clicking on the **Code Files** button on the book's webpage at the Packt Publishing website. This page can be accessed by entering the book's name in the **Search** box. Please note that you need to be logged in to your Packt account.

Once the file is downloaded, please make sure that you unzip or extract the folder using the latest version of:

- WinRAR / 7-Zip for Windows
- Zipeg / iZip / UnRarX for Mac
- 7-Zip / PeaZip for Linux

The code bundle for the book is also hosted on GitHub at https://github.com/PacktPublishing/Linux-Shell-Scripting-Bootcamp. We also have other code bundles from our rich catalog of books and videos available at https://github.com/PacktPublishing/. Check them out!

Errata

Although we have taken every care to ensure the accuracy of our content, mistakes do happen. If you find a mistake in one of our books—maybe a mistake in the text or the code—we would be grateful if you could report this to us. By doing so, you can save other readers from frustration and help us improve subsequent versions of this book. If you find any errata, please report them by visiting `http://www.packtpub.com/submit-errata`, selecting your book, clicking on the **Errata Submission Form** link, and entering the details of your errata. Once your errata are verified, your submission will be accepted and the errata will be uploaded to our website or added to any list of existing errata under the Errata section of that title.

To view the previously submitted errata, go to `https://www.packtpub.com/books/content/support` and enter the name of the book in the search field. The required information will appear under the **Errata** section.

Piracy

Piracy of copyrighted material on the Internet is an ongoing problem across all media. At Packt, we take the protection of our copyright and licenses very seriously. If you come across any illegal copies of our works in any form on the Internet, please provide us with the location address or website name immediately so that we can pursue a remedy.

Please contact us at `copyright@packtpub.com` with a link to the suspected pirated material.

We appreciate your help in protecting our authors and our ability to bring you valuable content.

Questions

If you have a problem with any aspect of this book, you can contact us at `questions@packtpub.com`, and we will do our best to address the problem.

1
Getting Started with Shell Scripting

This chapter is a brief introduction to shell scripting. It will assume the reader is mostly familiar with script basics and will serve as a refresher.

The topics covered in this chapter are as follows:

- The general format of a script.
- How to make a file executable.
- Creating a good Usage message and handling return codes.
- Show how to pass parameters from the command line.
- Show how to validate parameters by using conditional statements.
- Explain how to determine the attributes of files.

Getting started

You will always be able to create these scripts under a guest account, and most will run from there. It will be clearly stated when root access is needed to run a particular script.

The book will assume that the user has put a (.) at the beginning of the path for that account. If not, to run a script prepend . / to the filename. For example:

```
$ ./runme
```

The scripts will be made executable using the chmod command.

It is suggested that the user create a directory under his guest account specifically for the examples in this book. For example, something like this works well:

```
$ /home/guest1/LinuxScriptingBook/chapters/chap1
```

Of course, feel free to use whatever works best for you.

Following the general format of a bash script the very first line will contain this and nothing else:

```
#!/bin/sh
```

Note that in every other case text following the # sign is treated as comments.

For example,

This entire line is a comment

```
chmod 755 filename    # This text after the # is a comment
```

Use comments however you deem appropriate. Some people comment every line, some don't comment anything. I try to strike a balance somewhere in the middle of those two extremes.

Using a good text editor

I have found that most people are comfortable using vi to create and edit text documents under a UNIX/Linux environment. This is fine as vi is a very dependable application. I would suggest not using any type of word processing program, even if it claims to have a code development option. These programs might still put invisible control characters in the file which will probably cause the script to fail. This can take hours or even days to figure out unless you are good at looking at binary files.

Also, in my opinion, if you plan to do a lot of script and/or code development I suggest looking at some other text editor other than vi. You will almost certainly become more productive.

Demonstrating the use of scripts

Here is an example of a very simple script. It might not look like much but this is the basis for every script:

Chapter 1 - Script 1

```
#!/bin/sh
#
#  03/27/2017
#
exit 0
```

 By convention, in this book the script lines will usually be numbered. This is for teaching purposes only, in an actual script the lines are not numbered.

Here is the same script with the lines numbered:

```
1   #!/bin/sh
2   #
3   # 03/27/2017
4   #
5   exit 0
6
```

Here is an explanation for each line:

- Line 1 tells the operating system which shell interpreter to use. Note that on some distributions /bin/sh is actually a symbolic link to the interpreter.
- Lines that begin with a # are comments. Also, anything after a # is also treated as a comment.
- It is good practice to include a date in your scripts, either here in the comments section and/or in the Usage section (covered next).
- Line 5 is the return code from this script. This is optional but highly recommended.
- Line 6 is a blank line and is the last line of the script.

Using your favorite text editor, edit a new file named script1 and copy the preceding script without the line numbers into it. Save the file.

To make the file into an executable script run this:

```
$ chmod 755 script1
```

Now run the script:

```
$ script1
```

If you did not prepend a . to your path as mentioned in the introduction then run:

```
$ ./script1
```

Now check the return code:

```
$ echo $?
0
```

Here is a script that does something a little more useful:

Chapter 1 - Script 2

```
#!/bin/sh
#
# 3/26/2017
#
ping -c 1 google.com          # ping google.com just 1 time
echo Return code: $?
```

The ping command returns a zero on success and non-zero on failure. As you can see, echoing $? shows the return value of the command preceding it. More on this later.

Now let's pass a parameter and include a Usage statement:

Chapter 1 - Script 3

```
 1  #!/bin/sh
 2  #
 3  # 6/13/2017
 4  #
 5  if [ $# -ne 1 ] ; then
 6    echo "Usage: script3 file"
 7    echo " Will determine if the file exists."
 8    exit 255
 9  fi
10
```

```
11   if [ -f $1 ] ; then
12     echo File $1 exists.
13     exit 0
14   else
15     echo File $1 does not exist.
16     exit 1
17   fi
18
```

Here is an explanation for each line:

- Line 5 checks to see if a parameter was given. If not, lines 6 through 9 are executed. Note that is it usually a good idea to include an informative Usage statement in your script. It is also good to provide a meaningful return code.

- Line 11 checks to see if the file exists and if so lines 12-13 are executed. Otherwise lines 14-17 are run.

- A word about return codes: It is standard practice under Linux/UNIX to return zero if the command was successful, and non-zero if not. In this way the code returned can mean something useful, not only to humans, but to other scripts and programs as well. However, it is not mandatory to do this. If you want your script to return codes that are not errors but indicate some other condition by all means do so.

This next script expands on this topic:

Chapter 1 - Script 4

```
1    #!/bin/sh
2    #
3    # 6/13/2017
4    #
5    if [ $# -ne 1 ] ; then
6      echo "Usage: script4 filename"
7      echo " Will show various attributes of the file given."
8      exit 255
9    fi
10
11   echo -n "$1 "               # Stay on the line
12
```

```
13   if [ ! -e $1 ] ; then
14     echo does not exist.
15     exit 1                          # Leave script now
16   fi
17
18   if [ -f $1 ] ; then
19     echo is a file.
20   elif [ -d $1 ] ; then
21     echo is a directory.
22   fi
23
24   if [ -x $1 ] ; then
25     echo Is executable.
26   fi
27
28   if [ -r $1 ] ; then
29     echo Is readable.
30   else
31     echo Is not readable.
32   fi
33
34   if [ -w $1 ] ; then
35     echo Is writable.
36   fi
37
38   if [ -s $1 ] ; then
39     echo Is not empty.
40   else
41     echo Is empty.
42   fi
43
44   exit 0                            # No error
45
```

Here is an explanation for each line:

- Lines 5-9: If the script is not run with a parameter display the Usage message and exit with a return code of 255.
- Line 11 shows how to echo a string of text but still stay on the line (no linefeed).
- Line 13 shows how to determine if the parameter given is an existing file.
- Line 15 leaves the script as there is no reason to continue if the file doesn't exist.

The meaning of the remaining lines can be determined by the script itself. Note that there are many other checks that can be performed on a file, these are just a few.

Here are some examples of running script4 on my system:

```
guest1 $ script4
Usage: script4 filename
 Will show various attributes of the file given.


guest1 $ script4 /tmp
/tmp is a directory.
Is executable.
Is readable.
Is writable.
Is not empty.


guest1 $ script4 script4.numbered
script4.numbered is a file.
Is readable.
Is not empty.


guest1 $ script4 /usr
/usr is a directory.
Is executable.
Is readable.
Is not empty.


guest1 $ script4 empty1
```

```
empty1 is a file.
Is readable.
Is writable.
Is empty.

guest1 $ script4 empty-noread
empty-noread is a file.
Is not readable.
Is empty.
```

This next script shows how to determine the number of parameters that were passed to it:

Chapter 1 - Script 5

```
#!/bin/sh
#
# 3/27/2017
#
echo The number of parameters is: $#
exit 0
```

Let's try a few examples:

```
guest1 $ script5
The number of parameters is: 0

guest1 $ script5 parm1
The number of parameters is: 1

guest1 $ script5 parm1 Hello
The number of parameters is: 2

guest1 $ script5 parm1 Hello 15
The number of parameters is: 3

guest1 $ script5 parm1 Hello 15 "A string"
```

```
The number of parameters is: 4


guest1 $ script5 parm1 Hello 15 "A string" lastone
The number of parameters is: 5
```

 Remember that a quoted string is counted as 1 parameter. This is a way to pass strings that contain blank characters.

This next script shows how to handle multiple parameters in more detail:

Chapter 1 - Script 6

```
#!/bin/sh
#
# 3/27/2017
#

if [ $# -ne 3 ] ; then
  echo "Usage: script6 parm1 parm2 parm3"
  echo " Please enter 3 parameters."

  exit 255
fi

echo Parameter 1: $1
echo Parameter 2: $2
echo Parameter 3: $3

exit 0
```

The lines of this script were not numbered as it is rather simple. The $# contains the number of parameters that were passed to the script.

Summary

In this chapter we looked at the basics of script design. How to make a script executable was shown as was creating an informative Usage message. The importance of return codes was also covered as was the use and validation of parameters.

The next chapter will go into more detail about variables and conditional statements.

2
Working with Variables

This chapter will show how variables are used in a Linux system and in scripts.

The topics covered in this chapter are:

- Using variables in scripts
- Validating parameters using conditional statements
- Comparison operators for strings
- Environment variables

Using variables in scripts

A variable is simply a placeholder for some value. The value can change; however, the variable name will always be the same. Here is a simple example:

```
a=1
```

This assigns the value 1 to variable a. Here's another one:

```
b=2
```

To display what a variable contains use the echo statement:

```
echo Variable a is: $a
```

 Notice the $ preceding the variable name. This is required in order to show the contents of the variable.

If at anytime, you aren't seeing the results you expect first check for the $.

Here's an example using the command line:

```
$ a=1
$ echo a
a
$ echo $a
1
$ b="Jim"
$ echo b
b
$ echo $b
Jim
```

All variables in a Bash script are considered to be strings. This is different than in a programming language such as C, where everything is strongly typed. In the preceding example, a and b are strings even though they appear to be integers.

Here's a short script to get us started:

Chapter 2 - Script 1

```
#!/bin/sh
#
# 6/13/2017
#
echo "script1"

# Variables
a="1"
b=2
c="Jim"
d="Lewis"
e="Jim Lewis"
pi=3.141592

# Statements
echo $a
echo $b
echo $c
```

```
echo $d
echo $e
echo $pi
echo "End of script1"
```

And here is the output when run on my system:

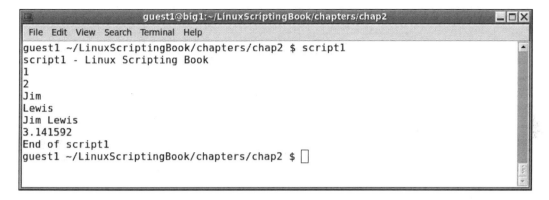

Since all of the variables are strings I could have also done this:

```
a="1"
b="2"
```

It is important to quote strings when they contain blank spaces such as variables d and e here.

I have found if I quote all the strings in my programs, but not the numbers, it is easier to keep track of how I am using the variable (that is, as a string or a number).

Validating parameters using conditional statements

Variables can be tested and compared against other variables when using a variable as a number.

Here is a list of some of the operators that can be used:

Operator	Description
-eq	This stands for equal to

Operator	Description
-ne	This stands for not equal to
-gt	This stands for greater than
-lt	This stands for less than
-ge	This stands for greater than or equal to
-le	This stands for less than or equal to
!	This stands for the negation operator

Let's take a look at this in our next example script:

Chapter 2 - Script 2

```
#!/bin/sh
#
# 6/13/2017
#
echo "script2"

# Numeric variables
a=100
b=100
c=200
d=300

echo a=$a b=$b c=$c d=$d      # display the values

# Conditional tests
if [ $a -eq $b ] ; then
  echo a equals b
fi

if [ $a -ne $b ] ; then
  echo a does not equal b
fi
```

```
if [ $a -gt $c ] ; then
 echo a is greater than c
fi


if [ $a -lt $c ] ; then
 echo a is less than c
fi


if [ $a -ge $d ] ; then
 echo a is greater than or equal to d
fi


if [ $a -le $d ] ; then
 echo a is less than or equal to d
fi


echo Showing the negation operator:
if [ ! $a -eq $b ] ; then
 echo Clause 1
else
 echo Clause 2
fi
echo "End of script2"
```

And the output is as follows:

```
guest1@big1:~/LinuxScriptingBook/chapters/chap2
File  Edit  View  Search  Terminal  Help
guest1 ~/LinuxScriptingBook/chapters/chap2 $ script2
script2 - Linux Scripting Book
a=100 b=100 c=200 d=300
a equals b
a is less than c
a is less than or equal to d
Showing the negation operator:
Clause 2
End of script2
guest1 ~/LinuxScriptingBook/chapters/chap2 $
```

To help understand this chapter run the script on your system. Try changing the values of the variables to see how it affects the output.

We saw the negation operator in *Chapter 1, Getting Started with Shell Scripting* when we were looking at files. As a reminder, it negates the expression. You could also say it does the opposite of what the original statement means.

Consider the following example:

```
a=1
b=1
if [ $a -eq $b ] ; then
  echo Clause 1
else
  echo Clause 2
fi
```

When this script is run it will display `Clause 1`. Now consider this:

```
a=1
b=1
if [ ! $a -eq $b ] ; then      # negation
  echo Clause 1
else
  echo Clause 2
fi
```

Because of the negation operator it will now display `Clause 2`. Try it on your system.

Comparison operators for strings

The comparison for strings are different than for numbers. Here is a partial list:

Operator	Explanation
=	This stands for equal to
!=	This stands for not equal to
>	This stands for greater than
<	This stands for less than

Now let's take a look at *Script 3*:

Chapter 2 - Script 3

```
1   #!/bin/sh
2   #
3   # 6/13/2017
4   #
5   echo "script3"
6
7   # String variables
8   str1="Kirk"
9   str2="Kirk"
10  str3="Spock"
11  str3="Dr. McCoy"
12  str4="Engineer Scott"
13  str5="A"
14  str6="B"
15
16  echo str1=$str1 str2=$str2 str3=$str3 str4=$str4
17
18  if [ "$str1" = "$str2" ] ; then
19    echo str1 equals str2
20  else
21    echo str1 does not equal str2
22  fi
23
24  if [ "$str1" != "$str2" ] ; then
25    echo str1 does not equal str2
26  else
27    echo str1 equals str2
28  fi
29
30  if [ "$str1" = "$str3" ] ; then
31    echo str1 equals str3
```

```
32  else
33    echo str1 does not equal str3
34  fi
35
36  if [ "$str3" = "$str4" ] ; then
37    echo str3 equals str4
38  else
39    echo str3 does not equal str4
40  fi
41
42  echo str5=$str5 str6=$str6
43
44  if [ "$str5" \> "$str6" ] ; then          # must escape the >
45    echo str5 is greater than str6
46  else
47    echo str5 is not greater than str6
48  fi
49
50  if [[ "$str5" > "$str6" ]] ; then          # or use double brackets
51    echo str5 is greater than str6
52  else
53    echo str5 is not greater than str6
54  fi
55
56  if [[ "$str5" < "$str6" ]] ; then          # double brackets
57    echo str5 is less than str6
58  else
59    echo str5 is not less than str6
60  fi
61
62  if [ -n "$str1" ] ; then      # test if str1 is not null
63    echo str1 is not null
64  fi
65
66  if [ -z "$str7" ] ; then      # test if str7 is null
```

```
67   echo str7 is null
68   fi
69   echo "End of script3"
70
```

Here's the output from my system:

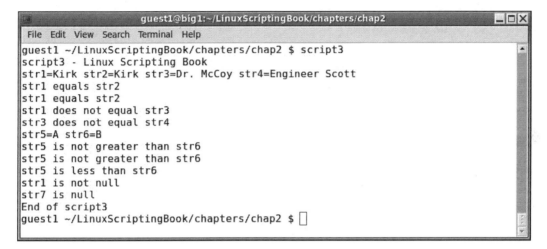

Lets go through this line by line:

- Lines 7-14 set up the variables
- Line 16 displays their values
- Line 18 checks for equality
- Line 24 uses the not equal operator
- The lines up to 50 are self-explanatory
- Line 44 needs some clarification. In order to avoid a syntax error the > and < operators must be escaped
- That is accomplished by using the backslash (or escape) \ character
- Line 50 shows how double brackets can be used to handle the greater than operator. As you can see in line 58 it works for the less than operator as well. My preference will be to use double brackets when needed.
- Line 62 shows how to check to see if a string is not null.
- And Line 66 shows how to check to see if a string is null.

Take a look at this script carefully to make sure it is clear to you. Also notice that str7 is shown to be null, but we didn't actually declare a str7. That is okay to do in a script, it will not generate an error. However, as a general rule of programming it is a good idea to declare all variables before they are used. Your code will be easier to understand and debug by you and others.

A scenario that comes up often in programming is when there are multiple conditions to test. For example, if something is true and something else is true take this action. This is accomplished by using the logical operators.

Here is *Script 4* to show how logical operators are used:

Chapter 2 - Script 4

```
#!/bin/sh
#
# 5/1/2017
#
echo "script4 - Linux Scripting Book"

if [ $# -ne 4 ] ; then
  echo "Usage: script4 number1 number2 number3 number4"
  echo "       Please enter 4 numbers."

  exit 255
fi


echo Parameters: $1 $2 $3 $4


echo Showing logical AND
if [[ $1 -eq $2 && $3 -eq $4 ]] ; then      # logical AND
  echo Clause 1
else
  echo Clause 2
fi


echo Showing logical OR
if [[ $1 -eq $2 || $3 -eq $4 ]] ; then      # logical OR
```

```
 echo Clause 1
else
 echo Clause 2
fi

echo "End of script4"
exit 0
```

Here's the output on my system:

```
guest1@big1:~/LinuxScriptingBook/chapters/chap2
File  Edit  View  Search  Terminal  Help
guest1 ~/LinuxScriptingBook/chapters/chap2 $ script4
script4 - Linux Scripting Book
Usage: script4 number1 number2 number3 number4
       Please enter 4 numbers.
guest1 ~/LinuxScriptingBook/chapters/chap2 $ script4 1 1 1 1
script4 - Linux Scripting Book
Parameters: 1 1 1 1
Showing logical AND
Clause 1
Showing logical OR
Clause 1
End of script4
guest1 ~/LinuxScriptingBook/chapters/chap2 $ script4 1 1 2 2
script4 - Linux Scripting Book
Parameters: 1 1 2 2
Showing logical AND
Clause 1
Showing logical OR
Clause 1
End of script4
guest1 ~/LinuxScriptingBook/chapters/chap2 $ script4 1 1 2 3
script4 - Linux Scripting Book
Parameters: 1 1 2 3
Showing logical AND
Clause 2
Showing logical OR
Clause 1
End of script4
guest1 ~/LinuxScriptingBook/chapters/chap2 $ script4 1 2 3 4
script4 - Linux Scripting Book
Parameters: 1 2 3 4
Showing logical AND
Clause 2
Showing logical OR
Clause 2
End of script4
guest1 ~/LinuxScriptingBook/chapters/chap2 $ []
```

Run this script on your system using several different parameters. On each attempt, try to determine what the output will be and then run it. Do this as many times as it takes until you can get it right every time. Understanding this concept now will be very helpful as we get into more complicated scripts later.

Now let's look *Script 5* to see how math can be performed:

Chapter 2 - Script 5

```
#!/bin/sh
#
# 5/1/2017
#
echo "script5 - Linux Scripting Book"

num1=1
num2=2
num3=0
num4=0
sum=0

echo num1=$num1
echo num2=$num2

let sum=num1+num2
echo "The sum is: $sum"

let num1++
echo "num1 is now: $num1"

let num2--
echo "num2 is now: $num2"

let num3=5
echo num3=$num3

let num3=num3+10
```

```
echo "num3 is now: $num3"


let num3+=10
echo "num3 is now: $num3"


let num4=50
echo "num4=$num4"


let num4-=10
echo "num4 is now: $num4"


echo "End of script5"
```

And here is the output:

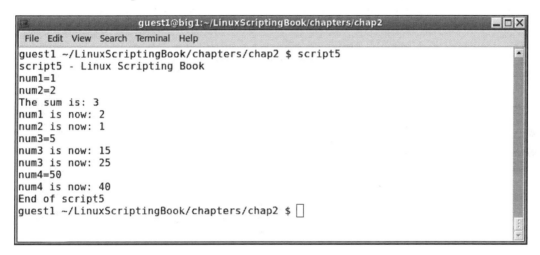

As you can see, the variables are set up as before. The let command is used to perform math. Note the $ prefix is not used:

```
let sum=num1+num2
```

Also note the shorthand way of doing some operations. For example, say you want to increment the var num1 by 1. You could do this as follows:

```
let num1=num1+1
```

Alternatively, you could use the shorthand notation:

```
let num1++
```

Run this script and change some of the values to get a feel for how the math operations work. We will go over this in much more detail in a later chapter.

Environment variables

So far we have only talked about variables that are local to a script. There are also system wide environment variables (env vars) which play a very important part of any Linux system. Here are a few, some of which the reader may already be aware of:

Variable	Role
HOME	user's home directory
PATH	directories which are searched for commands
PS1	command line prompt
HOSTNAME	hostname of the machine
SHELL	shell that is being used
USER	user of this session
EDITOR	text editor to use for crontab and other programs
HISTSIZE	number of commands that will be shown by the history command
TERM	type of command line terminal that is being used

Most of these are self-explanatory, however, I will mention a few.

The PS1 environment variable controls what the shell prompt displays as part of the command line. The default setting is usually something like [guest1@big1 ~]$, which is not as useful as it could be. At a minimum, a good prompt shows at least the hostname and current directory.

For example, as I work on this chapter the prompt on my system looks just like this:

```
big1 ~/LinuxScriptingBook/chapters/chap2 $
```

big1 is the hostname of my system and ~/LinuxScriptingBook/chapters/chap2 is the current directory. Recall that the tilde ~ stands for the user's home directory; so in my case this expands out to:

```
/home/guest1/LinuxScriptingBook/chapters/chap2
```

The "$" means I am running under a guest account.

To enable this, my PS1 env var is defined in /home/guest1/.bashrc as follows:

```
export PS1="\h \w $ "
```

The "\h" shows the hostname and the \w shows the current directory. This is a very useful prompt and I have been using it for many years. Here's how to show the username as well:

```
export PS1="\u \h \w $ "
```

The prompt would now look like this:

```
guest1 big1 ~/LinuxScriptingBook/chapters/chap2 $
```

If you change the PS1 variable in your .bashrc file, make certain you do it after any other lines that are already in the file.

For example, here is what my original .bashrc contains under my guest1 account:

```
# .bashrc


# Source global definitions
if [ -f /etc/bashrc ]; then
    . /etc/bashrc
fi


# User specific aliases and functions
```

Put your PS1 definition after these lines.

> If you log into a lot of different machines on a daily basis, there is a PS1 trick I have found that is very useful. This will be shown in a later chapter.
>
> You may have noticed that it looks as though I did not always use a good PS1 variable for the examples in this book. It was edited out during book creation to save space.

The EDITOR variable can be very useful. This tells the system which text editor to use for things such as editing the user's crontab (crontab -e). If not set, it defaults to the vi editor. It can be changed by putting it in the user's .bashrc file. Here is what mine looks like for the root account:

```
export EDITOR=/lewis/bin64/kw
```

When I run crontab -l (or -e), my personally written text editor comes up instead of vi. Very handy!

Here we'll take a look at *Script 6*, that shows some of the variables on my system under my `guest1` account:

Chapter 2 - Script 6

```sh
#!/bin/sh
#
# 5/1/2017
#
echo "script6 - Linux Scripting Book"

echo HOME - $HOME
echo PATH - $PATH
echo HOSTNAME - $HOSTNAME
echo SHELL - $SHELL
echo USER - $USER
echo EDITOR - $EDITOR
echo HISTSIZE - $HISTSIZE
echo TERM - $TERM


echo "End of script6"
```

Here's the output:

```
guest1@big1:~/LinuxScriptingBook/chapters/chap2                    _ □ X
 File  Edit  View  Search  Terminal  Help
guest1 ~/LinuxScriptingBook/chapters/chap2 $ script6
script6 - Linux Scripting Book
HOME - /home/guest1
PATH - .:/usr/lib64/qt-3.3/bin:/usr/local/bin:/bin:/usr/bin:/usr/local/sbin:/usr
/sbin:/sbin:/home/guest1/bin
HOSTNAME - big1.com
SHELL - /bin/bash
USER - guest1
EDITOR - /home/guest1/bin/kw
HISTSIZE - 5000
TERM - xterm
End of script6
guest1 ~/LinuxScriptingBook/chapters/chap2 $ □
```

You can also create and use your own env vars. This is a really powerful feature of a Linux system. Here are some examples that I use in my /root/.bashrc file:

```
BIN=/lewis/bin64
DOWN=/home/guest1/Downloads
DESK=/home/guest1/Desktop
JAVAPATH=/usr/lib/jvm/java-1.7.0-openjdk-1.7.0.99.x86_64/include/
KW_WORKDIR=/root
L1=guest1@192.168.1.21
L4=guest1@192.168.1.2
LBCUR=/home/guest1/LinuxScriptingBook/chapters/chap2
export BIN DOWN DESK JAVAPATH KW_WORKDIR L1 L4 LBCUR
```

- BIN: This is the directory of my executables and scripts under root
- DOWN: This is the download directory for email attachments, etc
- DESK: This is the download directory for screenshots
- JAVAPATH: This is the directory to use when I am writing Java apps
- KW_WORKDIR: This is where my editor puts its working files
- L1 and L2: This is the IP addresses to my laptops
- LBCUR: This is the current directory I am working in for this book

Be sure to export your variables so that they can be accessed by other terminals. Also remember to source your .bashrc when you make a change. On my system the command would be:

```
guest1 $ . /home/guest1/.bashrc
```

 Don't forget the period at the beginning of the command!

I will show in a later chapter how these env vars can be paired with aliases. For example, the bin command on my system is an alias that changes the current directory to the /lewis/bin64 directory. This is one of the most powerful features in a Linux system, however, I am always surprised that I do not see it used more often.

The last type of variable we will cover in this chapter is called an array. Suppose you want to write a script that contains all of the IP addresses of the machines in your lab. You could do something like this:

```
L0=192.168.1.1
L1=192.168.1.10
L2=192.168.1.15
L3=192.168.1.16
L4=192.168.1.20
L5=192.168.1.26
```

That will work and in fact I do something similar to that in my home office/lab. However, suppose you have a whole lot of machines. Using arrays can make your life a lot simpler.

Take a look at *Script 7*:

Chapter 2 - Script 7

```
#!/bin/sh
#
# 5/1/2017
#
echo "script7 - Linux Scripting Book"

array_var=(1 2 3 4 5 6)

echo ${array_var[0]}
echo ${array_var[1]}
echo ${array_var[2]}
echo ${array_var[3]}
echo ${array_var[4]}
echo ${array_var[5]}

echo "List all elements:"
echo ${array_var[*]}

echo "List all elements (alternative method):"
```

```
echo ${array_var[@]}

echo "Number of elements: ${#array_var[*]}"
labip[0]="192.168.1.1"
labip[1]="192.168.1.10"
labip[2]="192.168.1.15"
labip[3]="192.168.1.16"
labip[4]="192.168.1.20"

echo ${labip[0]}
echo ${labip[1]}
echo ${labip[2]}
echo ${labip[3]}
echo ${labip[4]}

echo "List all elements:"
echo ${labip[*]}

echo "Number of elements: ${#labip[*]}"
echo "End of script7"
```

And here is the output on my system:

```
guest1@big1:~/LinuxScriptingBook/chapters/chap2

File  Edit  View  Search  Terminal  Help
guest1 ~/LinuxScriptingBook/chapters/chap2 $ script7
script7 - Linux Scripting Book
1
2
3
4
5
6
List all elements:
1 2 3 4 5 6
List all elements (alternative method):
1 2 3 4 5 6
Number of elements: 6
192.168.1.1
192.168.1.10
192.168.1.15
192.168.1.16
192.168.1.20
List all elements:
192.168.1.1 192.168.1.10 192.168.1.15 192.168.1.16 192.168.1.20
Number of elements: 5
End of script7
guest1 ~/LinuxScriptingBook/chapters/chap2 $
```

Run this script on your system and try experimenting with it. If you have never seen or used an array before, don't let them scare you; you will get familiar with them soon enough. This is another area where it's easy to forget the `${ array variable here }` syntax so if the script doesn't do what you want (or generates an error) check that first.

We will talk about arrays again in much more detail when we cover loops in the next chapter.

Summary

In this chapter we covered how to declare and use both environment and local variables. We talked about how math is performed and how to work with arrays.

We also covered using variables in scripts. *Script 1* showed how to assign a variable and display its value. *Script 2* showed how to deal with numeric variables and *Script 3* showed how to compare strings. *Script 4* showed logical operators and *Script 5* showed how math can be performed. *Script 6* showed how environment variables are used and *Script 7* showed how to use arrays.

3
Using Loops and the sleep Command

This chapter shows how to use loops to perform iterative operations. It also shows how to create a delay in a script. The reader will learn how to use loops and the sleep command in a script.

Topics covered in this chapter are as follows:

- Standard for, while, and until loops.
- Nesting of loops, and how not to get confused.
- Introduce the sleep command and how it is used to cause a delay in a script.
- Go over a common pitfall of using sleep.

Using loops

One of the most important features of any programming language is the ability to perform a task, or tasks, a number of times and then stop when an ending condition is met. This is accomplished by using a loop.

The next section shows an example of a very simple while loop:

Chapter 3 - Script 1

```
#!/bin/sh
#
# 5/2/2017
#
echo "script1 - Linux Scripting Book"
```

```
x=1
while [ $x -le 10 ]
do
 echo x: $x
 let x++
done

echo "End of script1"

exit 0
```

And here is the output:

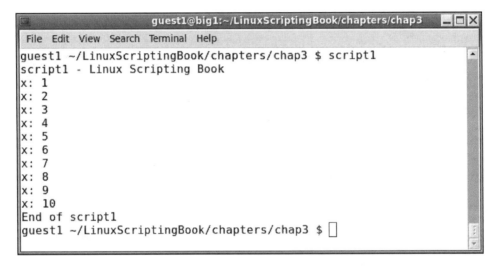

We start by setting variable x to 1. The while statement checks to see if x is less than or equal to 10 and if so, runs the commands between the do and done statements. It will continue to do this until x equals 11, in which case the lines after the done statement are then run.

Run this on your system. It is very important to understand this script so that we can move on to more advanced loops.

Let's look at another script in the next section—see if you can determine what is wrong with it.

Chapter 3 - Script 2

```
#!/bin/sh
#
# 5/2/2017
#
echo "script2 - Linux Scripting Book"

x=1
while [ $x -ge 0 ]
do
  echo x: $x
  let x++
done

echo "End of script2"

exit 0
```

Feel free to skip the running of this one unless you really want to. Look carefully at the `while` test. It says while x is greater than or equal to 0, run the commands inside the loop. Is x ever going to not meet this condition? No, it is not, and this is what is known as an infinite loop. Don't worry; you can still end the script by pressing *Ctrl* + *C* (hold down the *Ctrl* key and press *C*). This will terminate the script.

I wanted to cover infinite loops right away as you will almost certainly do this from time to time, and I wanted you to know how to terminate the script when it happens. I certainly did this a few times when I was first starting out.

Okay let's do something more useful. Suppose you are starting a new project and need to create some directories on your system. You could do it one command at a time, or use a loop in a script.

We'll a look at this in *Script 3*.

Chapter 3 - Script 3

```sh
#!/bin/sh
#
# 5/2/2017
#
echo "script3 - Linux Scripting Book"

x=1
while [ $x -le 10 ]
do
 echo x=$x
 mkdir chapter$x
 let x++
done
echo "End of script3"

exit 0
```

This simple script assumes you are starting at the base directory. When run it will create directories chapter 1 through chapter 10 and then proceed to the end.

When running scripts that make changes to your computer, it is a good idea to make sure the logic is correct before running it for real. For example, before running this I commented out the mkdir line. I then ran the script to make sure it stopped after it displayed that x was equal to 10. I then uncommented the line and ran it for real.

Screen manipulation

We'll see another script in the next section that uses a loop to put text on the screen:

Chapter 3 - Script 4

```
#!/bin/sh
#
# 5/2/2017
#
echo "script4 - Linux Scripting Book"

if [ $# -ne 1 ] ; then
 echo "Usage: script4 string"
 echo "Will display the string on every line."
 exit 255
fi

tput clear                  # clear the screen

x=1
while [ $x -le $LINES ]
do
 echo "********** $1 **********"
 let x++
done

exit 0
```

Before executing this script run the following command:

```
echo $LINES
```

If the number of lines in that terminal is not displayed run the following command:

```
export LINES=$LINES
```

Then proceed to run the script. The following is the output on my system when run with `script4 Linux`:

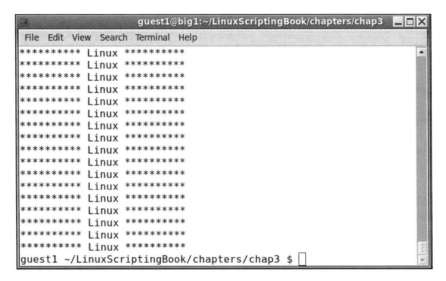

Okay, so I agree this might not be terribly useful, but it does show a few things. The LINES env var contains the current number of lines (or rows) in the current terminal. This can be useful for limiting output in more complex scripts and that will be shown in a later chapter. This example also shows how the screen can be manipulated in a script.

If you needed to export the LINES variable, you may want to put it in your `.bashrc` file and re-source it.

We'll take a look at another script in the next section:

Chapter 3 - Script 5

```
#!/bin/sh
#
# 5/2/2017
#
# script5 - Linux Scripting Book


tput clear                 # clear the screen


row=1
```

```
while [ $row -le $LINES ]
do
 col=1
 while [ $col -le $COLUMNS ]
 do
  echo -n "#"
  let col++
 done
 echo ""                        # output a carriage return
 let row++
done


exit 0
```

This is similar to *Script 4* in that it shows how to display output within the confines of the terminal. Note, you may have to export the COLUMNS env var like we did with the LINES var.

You probably noticed something a little different in this script. There is a while statement inside a while statement. This is called a nested loop and is used very frequently in programming.

We start by declaring row=1 and then begin the outer while loop. The col var is then set to 1 and then the inner loop is started. This inner loop is what displays the character on each column of the line. When the end of the line is reached, the loop ends and the echo statement outputs a carriage return. The row var is incremented, and then the process starts again. It ends after the last line.

By using the LINES and COLUMNS env vars only the actual screen is written to. You can test this by running the program and then expanding the terminal.

When using nested loops it can be easy to get mixed up about what goes where. Here is something I try to do every time. When I first realize a loop is going to be needed in a program (which can be a script, C, or Java, and so on), I code the loop body first like this:

```
while [ condition ]
do
    other statements will go here
done
```

This way I don't forget the `done` statement and it's also lined up correctly. If I then need another loop I just do it again:

```
while [ condition ]
do
   while [ condition ]
   do
      other statements will go here
   done
done
```

You can nest as many loops as you need.

Indenting your code

This is probably a good time to talk about indenting. In the past (that is, 30+ years ago) everyone used a text editor with a mono-spaced font to write their code and so it was relatively easy to keep everything lined up with just a one space indent. Later, when people started using word processors with a variable pitched font, it became harder to see the indentation and so more spaces (or tabs) were used. My suggestion is to use what you feel most comfortable with. However, with that said you may have to learn to read and use whatever code style that is in place for your company.

So far we have only talked about the `while` statement. Now let's look at an `until` loop in the next section:

Chapter 3 - Script 6

```
#!/bin/sh
#
# 5/3/2017
#
echo "script6 - Linux Scripting Book"

echo "This shows the while loop"

x=1
while [ $x -lt 11 ]          # perform the loop while the condition
do                           # is true
```

```
  echo "x: $x"
  let x++
done

echo "This shows the until loop"

x=1
until [ $x -gt 10 ]          # perform the loop until the condition
do                           # is true
  echo "x: $x"
  let x++
done

echo "End of script6"

exit 0
```

The output:

```
guest1@big1:~/LinuxScriptingBook/chapters/chap3
 File  Edit  View  Search  Terminal  Help
guest1 ~/LinuxScriptingBook/chapters/chap3 $ script6
script6 - Linux Scripting Book
This shows the while loop
x: 1
x: 2
x: 3
x: 4
x: 5
x: 6
x: 7
x: 8
x: 9
x: 10
This shows the until loop
x: 1
x: 2
x: 3
x: 4
x: 5
x: 6
x: 7
x: 8
x: 9
x: 10
End of script6
guest1 ~/LinuxScriptingBook/chapters/chap3 $
```

Take a look at this script. The output from both loops is the same; however, the conditions are the opposite. The first loop continues while the condition is true, the second loop continues until the condition is true. A not-so-subtle difference so be on the watch for that.

Using the for statement

Another way to loop is to use the for statement. It is commonly used when working with files and other lists. The general syntax of a for loop is as follows:

```
for variable in list
do
    some commands
done
```

The list can be a collection of strings, or a filename wildcard, and so on. We can take a look at this in the example given in the next section.

Chapter 3 - Script 7

```
#!/bin/sh
#
# 5/4/2017
#
echo "script7 - Linux Scripting Book"

for i in jkl.c bob Linux "Hello there" 1 2 3
do
  echo -n "$i "
done

for i in script*              # returns the scripts in this directory
do
  echo $i
done

echo "End of script7"
exit 0
```

And the output on my system. This is my `chap3` directory:

```
guest1@big1:~/LinuxScriptingBook/chapters/chap3        _□✕
File  Edit  View  Search  Terminal  Help
guest1 ~/LinuxScriptingBook/chapters/chap3 $ script7
script7 - Linux Scripting Book
jkl.c bob Linux Hello there 1 2 3 script1
script10
script11
script12
script2
script3
script4
script5
script6
script7
script8
script9
End of script7
guest1 ~/LinuxScriptingBook/chapters/chap3 $ □
```

The next script shows how the `for` statement can be used with files:

Chapter 3 - Script 8

```sh
#!/bin/sh
#
# 5/3/2017
#
echo "script8 - Linux Scripting Book"

if [ $# -eq 0 ] ; then
 echo "Please enter at least 1 parameter."
 exit 255
fi

for i in $*              # the "$*" returns every parameter given
do                       # to the script
 echo -n "$i "
done

echo ""                  # carriage return
echo "End of script8"

exit 0
```

The following is the output:

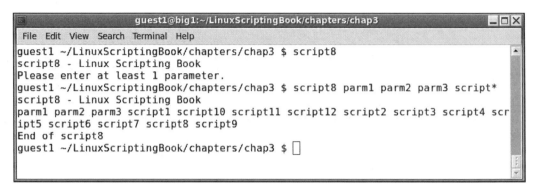

There are a few other things you can do with the for statement, consult the man page of Bash for more information.

Leaving a loop early

Sometimes when you are coding a script, you encounter a situation where you would like to exit the loop early, before the ending condition is met. This can be accomplished using the break and continue commands.

Here is a script that shows these commands. I am also introducing the sleep command which will be talked about in detail in the next script.

Chapter 3 - Script 9

```
#!/bin/sh
#
# 5/3/2017
#
echo "script9 - Linux Scripting Book"

FN1=/tmp/break.txt
FN2=/tmp/continue.txt

x=1
```

```
while [ $x -le 1000000 ]
do
 echo "x:$x"
 if [ -f $FN1 ] ; then
  echo "Running the break command"
  rm -f $FN1
  break
 fi

 if [ -f $FN2 ] ; then
  echo "Running the continue command"
  rm -f $FN2
  continue
 fi

 let x++
 sleep 1
done

echo "x:$x"

echo "End of script9"

exit 0
```

Here's the output from my system:

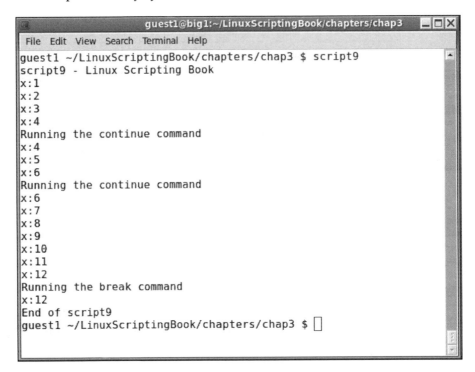

Run this on your system, and in another terminal cd to the /tmp directory. Run the command touch continue.txt and watch what happens. If you like you can do this multiple times (remember that up arrow recalls the previous command). Notice how the variable x does not get incremented when the continue command is hit. This is because the control goes immediately back to the while statement.

Now run the touch break.txt command. The script will end, and again, x has not been incremented. This is because break immediately causes the loop to end.

The break and continue commands are used quite often in scripts and so be sure to play with this one enough to really understand what is going on.

The sleep command

I showed the sleep command earlier, let's look at that in much more detail. In general, the sleep command is used to introduce a delay in the script. For example, in the previous script if I had not used sleep the output would have scrolled off too quickly to see what was going on.

The `sleep` command takes a parameter indicating how long to make the delay. For example, `sleep 1` means to introduce a delay of one second. Here are a few examples:

```
sleep 1      # sleep 1 second (the default is seconds)
sleep 1s     # sleep 1 second
sleep 1m     # sleep 1 minute
sleep 1h     # sleep 1 hour
sleep 1d     # sleep 1 day
```

The `sleep` command actually has a bit more capability that what is shown here. For more information, please consult the `man` page (`man sleep`).

Here's a script showing in more detail how `sleep` works:

Chapter 3 - Script 10

```
#!/bin/sh
#
# 5/3/2017
#
echo "script10 - Linux Scripting Book"

echo "Sleeping seconds..."
x=1
while [ $x -le 5 ]
do
 date
 let x++
 sleep 1
done

echo "Sleeping minutes..."
x=1
while [ $x -le 2 ]
do
 date
 let x++
```

```
sleep 1m
done

echo "Sleeping hours..."
x=1
while [ $x -le 2 ]
do
 date
 let x++
 sleep 1h
done

echo "End of script10"
exit 0
```

And the output:

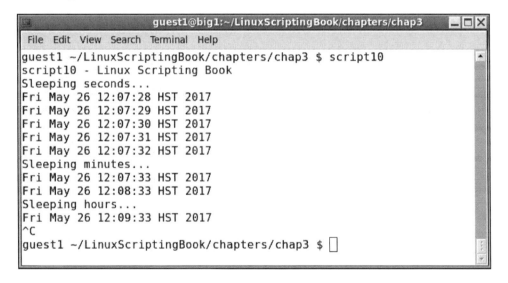

You may have noticed that I pressed *Ctrl* + *C* to terminate the script since I didn't want to wait 2 hours for it to finish. Scripts of this nature are used very extensively in a Linux system to monitor processes, watch for files, and so on.

There is a common pitfall when using the sleep command that needs to be mentioned.

 Remember that the sleep command introduces a delay into the script. To be clear, when you code a sleep 60 it means to introduce a delay of 60 seconds; it does not mean it is going to run the script every 60 seconds. There is a big difference.

We'll see an example of this in the following section:

Chapter 3 - Script 11

```sh
#!/bin/sh
#
# 5/3/2017
#
echo "script11 - Linux Scripting Book"

while [ true ]
do
 date
 sleep 60                    # 60 seconds
done

echo "End of script11"

exit 0
```

This is the output on my system. It doesn't take all that long to eventually get out of sync:

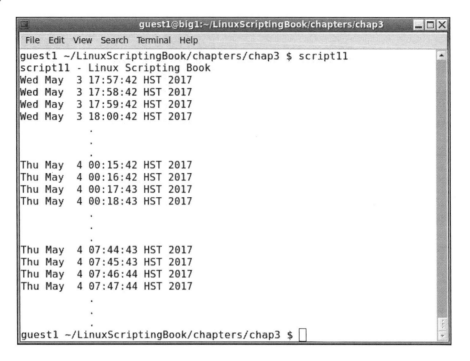

For the vast majority of scripts this is never going to be a problem. Just remember if what you are trying to accomplish is time critical, like trying to run a command at exactly 12:00 am every night, you might want to look at some other approach. Note that crontab will also not do this as there is about a 1 or 2 second delay before it runs the command.

Watching a process

There are a few more topics that we should look at in this chapter. Suppose you want to be alerted when a running process ends on your system.

Here's a script that notifies the user when the specified process ends. Note that there are other ways to do this task, this is just one approach.

Chapter 3 - Script 12

```
#!/bin/sh
#
# 5/3/2017
#
echo "script12 - Linux Scripting Book"

if [ $# -ne 1 ] ; then
 echo "Usage: script12 process-directory"
 echo " For example: script12 /proc/20686"
 exit 255
fi


FN=$1                       # process directory i.e. /proc/20686
rc=1
while [ $rc -eq 1 ]
do
 if [ ! -d $FN ] ; then     # if directory is not there
   echo "Process $FN is not running or has been terminated."
   let rc=0
 else
   sleep 1
 fi
done

echo "End of script12"
exit 0
```

To see this script in action run the following commands:

- In a terminal, run `script9`

- In another terminal run `ps auxw | grep script9`. The output will be something like this:

  ```
  guest1   20686  0.0  0.0 106112  1260 pts/34   S+   17:20   0:00 /
  bin/sh ./script9

  guest1   23334  0.0  0.0 103316   864 pts/18   S+   17:24   0:00
  grep script9
  ```

- Use the process ID from `script9` (in this case `20686`) and use it as the parameter to run `script12`:

  ```
  $ script12 /proc/20686
  ```

You may let it run for a bit if you want. Eventually go back to the terminal that is running `script9` and terminate it with *Ctrl + C*. You will see `script12` output a message and then also terminate. Feel free to experiment with this one as it has a lot of important information in it.

You may notice that in this script I used a variable, `rc`, to determine when to end the loop. I could have used the `break` command as we saw earlier in this chapter. However, using a control variable (as it's often called) is considered to be a better programming style.

A script like this can be very useful when you have started a command and then it takes longer than you expected for it to finish.

For example, a while back I started a format operation on an external 1 TB USB drive using the `mkfs` command. It took a few days to complete and I wanted to know exactly when so that I could continue working with the drive.

Creating numbered backup files

Now for a bonus here is a ready-to-run script that can be used to make numbered backup files. Before I came up with this (many years ago) I would go through the ritual of making the backup by hand. My numbering scheme was not always consistent, and I quickly realized it would be easier to have a script do it. This is something computers are really good at.

I call this script `cbs`. I wrote this so long ago I'm not even sure what it stands for. Maybe it was **Computer Backup Script** or something like that.

Chapter 3 – Script 13

```
#!/bin/sh
#
echo "cbS by Lewis 5/4/2017"

if [ $# -eq 0 ] ; then
 echo "Usage: cbS filename(s) "
 echo " Will make a numbered backup of the files(s) given."
 echo " Files must be in the current directory."
 exit 255
fi


rc=0                         # return code, default is no error
for fn in $*                 # for each filename given on the command
line
do
 if [ ! -f $fn ] ; then      # if not found
  echo "File $fn not found."
  rc=1                       # one or more files were not found
 else
  cnt=1                      # file counter
  loop1=0                    # loop flag
  while [ $loop1 -eq 0 ]
  do
   tmp=bak-$cnt.$fn
   if [ ! -f $tmp ] ; then
     cp $fn $tmp
     echo "File "$tmp" created."
     loop1=1                 # end the inner loop
   else
     let cnt++               # try the next one
   fi
  done
 fi
done

exit $rc                     # exit with return code
```

It starts with a Usage message as it needs at least one filename to work on.

Note that this command requires the files be in the current directory, so doing something like cbS /tmp/file1.txt will generate an error.

The rc variable is initialized to 0. If a file is not found, it will be set to 1.

Now let's look at the inner loop. The logic here is a backup file will be created from the original file using the cp command. The naming scheme for the backup file is bak-(number).original-filename where number is the next one in sequence. The code determines what the next number is by going through all of the bak-#. filename files until it doesn't find one. That one then becomes the new filename.

Get this one going on your system. Feel free to name it whatever you like, but be careful to name it something other than an existing Linux command. Use the which command to check.

Here is some example output on my system:

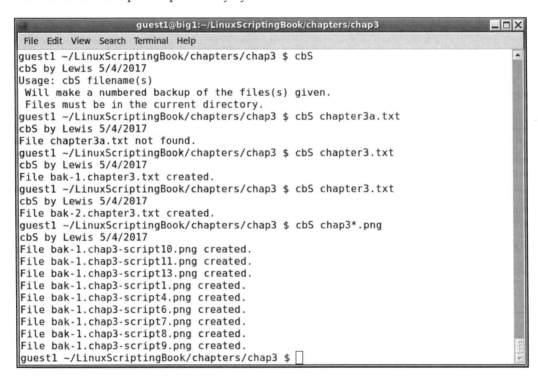

```
guest1@big1:~/LinuxScriptingBook/chapters/chap3
File  Edit  View  Search  Terminal  Help
guest1 ~/LinuxScriptingBook/chapters/chap3 $ cbS
cbS by Lewis 5/4/2017
Usage: cbS filename(s)
 Will make a numbered backup of the files(s) given.
 Files must be in the current directory.
guest1 ~/LinuxScriptingBook/chapters/chap3 $ cbS chapter3a.txt
cbS by Lewis 5/4/2017
File chapter3a.txt not found.
guest1 ~/LinuxScriptingBook/chapters/chap3 $ cbS chapter3.txt
cbS by Lewis 5/4/2017
File bak-1.chapter3.txt created.
guest1 ~/LinuxScriptingBook/chapters/chap3 $ cbS chapter3.txt
cbS by Lewis 5/4/2017
File bak-2.chapter3.txt created.
guest1 ~/LinuxScriptingBook/chapters/chap3 $ cbS chap3*.png
cbS by Lewis 5/4/2017
File bak-1.chap3-script10.png created.
File bak-1.chap3-script11.png created.
File bak-1.chap3-script13.png created.
File bak-1.chap3-script1.png created.
File bak-1.chap3-script4.png created.
File bak-1.chap3-script6.png created.
File bak-1.chap3-script7.png created.
File bak-1.chap3-script8.png created.
File bak-1.chap3-script9.png created.
guest1 ~/LinuxScriptingBook/chapters/chap3 $
```

This script could be greatly improved upon. It could be made to work with paths/files, and the cp command should be checked for errors. This level of coding will be covered in a later chapter.

Summary

In this chapter we covered the different types of loop statements and how they differ from each other. Nesting loops and the `sleep` command were also covered. The common pitfall when using the `sleep` command was also mentioned, and a backup script was introduced to show how to easily create numbered backup files.

In the next chapter we will go over the creation and calling of subroutines.

4
Creating and Calling Subroutines

This chapter shows how to create and call subroutines in a script.

The topics covered in this chapter are as follows:

- Show some simple subroutines.
- Show more advanced routines.
- Mention return codes again and how they work in scripts.

In the previous chapters we have seen mostly simple scripts that were not very complicated. Scripts can actually do a whole lot more which we are about to see.

First, let's start with a selection of simple but powerful scripts. These are mainly shown to give the reader an idea of just what can be done quickly with a script.

Clearing the screen

The `tput clear` terminal command can be used to clear the current command-line session. You could type `tput clear` all the time, but wouldn't just `cls` be nicer?

Here's a simple script that clears the current screen:

Chapter 4 - Script 1

```
#!/bin/sh
#
# 5/8/2017
#
tput clear
```

Notice that this was so simple I didn't even bother to include a `Usage` message or return code. Remember, to make this a command on your system do this:

- `cd $HOME/bin`
- create/edit a file named `cls`
- copy and paste the preceding code into this file
- save the file
- run `chmod 755 cls`

You can now type `cls` from any terminal (under that user) and your screen will clear. Try it.

File redirection

At this point we need to go over file redirection. This is the ability to have the output from a command or script be copied into a file instead of going to the screen. This is done by using the redirection operator, which is really just the greater than sign.

Here is the screenshot of some commands that were run on my system:

```
guest1@big1:~/LinuxScriptingBook/chapters/chap4

File  Edit  View  Search  Terminal  Help

guest1 ~/LinuxScriptingBook/chapters/chap4 $ ifconfig > ifconfig.txt
guest1 ~/LinuxScriptingBook/chapters/chap4 $ cat ifconfig.txt
eth0      Link encap:Ethernet  HWaddr E0:Z9:95:5B:BZ:87
          inet addr:192.168.1.20  Bcast:192.168.1.255  Mask:255.255.255.0
          inet6 addr: fe80::e269:95ff:fe5b:b687/64 Scope:Link
          UP BROADCAST RUNNING MULTICAST  MTU:1500  Metric:1
          RX packets:194702818 errors:0 dropped:30 overruns:0 frame:0
          TX packets:354190522 errors:0 dropped:0 overruns:0 carrier:0
          collisions:0 txqueuelen:1000
          RX bytes:146133079920 (136.0 GiB)  TX bytes:390554310707 (363.7 GiB)
          Interrupt:20 Memory:fbac0000-fbae0000

lo        Link encap:Local Loopback
          inet addr:127.0.0.1  Mask:255.0.0.0
          inet6 addr: ::1/128 Scope:Host
          UP LOOPBACK RUNNING  MTU:65536  Metric:1
          RX packets:253218017 errors:0 dropped:0 overruns:0 frame:0
          TX packets:253218017 errors:0 dropped:0 overruns:0 carrier:0
          collisions:0 txqueuelen:0
          RX bytes:19885357492 (18.5 GiB)  TX bytes:19885357492 (18.5 GiB)

virbr0    Link encap:Ethernet  HWaddr 52:Z4:00:EC:ZF:A9
          inet addr:192.168.122.1  Bcast:192.168.122.255  Mask:255.255.255.0
          UP BROADCAST RUNNING MULTICAST  MTU:1500  Metric:1
          RX packets:0 errors:0 dropped:0 overruns:0 frame:0
          TX packets:37 errors:0 dropped:0 overruns:0 carrier:0
          collisions:0 txqueuelen:0
          RX bytes:0 (0.0 b)  TX bytes:2200 (2.1 KiB)

guest1 ~/LinuxScriptingBook/chapters/chap4 $
```

As you can see, the output from the `ifconfig` command was sent (or redirected) to the `ifconfig.txt` file.

Command piping

Now let's look at command piping, which is the ability to run a command and have the output from it serve as the input to another command.

Suppose a program or script named `loop1` is running on your system and you want to know the PID of it. You could run the `ps auxw` command to a file, and then `grep` the file for `loop1`. Alternatively, you could do it in one step by using a pipe as follows:

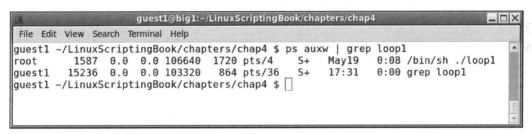

Pretty cool, right? This is a very powerful feature in a Linux system and is used extensively. We will be seeing a lot more of this soon.

The next section shows another very short script using some command piping. This clears the screen and then shows only the first 10 lines from `dmesg`:

Chapter 4 - Script 2

```
#!/bin/sh
#
# 5/8/2017
#
tput clear
dmesg | head
```

And here is the output:

```
guest1@big1:~/LinuxScriptingBook/chapters/chap4
File  Edit  View  Search  Terminal  Help
Initializing cgroup subsys cpuset
Initializing cgroup subsys cpu
Linux version 2.6.32-642.el6.x86_64 (mockbuild@worker1.bsys.centos.org) (gcc version
4.4.7 20120313 (Red Hat 4.4.7-17) (GCC) ) #1 SMP Tue May 10 17:27:01 UTC 2016
Command line: ro root=UUID=b92656f9-c523-4357-9313-77c2c80a7115 rd_NO_LUKS rd_NO_LVM
LANG=en_US.UTF-8 rd_NO_MD SYSFONT=latarcyrheb-sun16 crashkernel=128M  KEYBOARDTYPE=pc
 KEYTABLE=us rd_NO_DM rhgb quiet
KERNEL supported cpus:
  Intel GenuineIntel
  AMD AuthenticAMD
  Centaur CentaurHauls
BIOS-provided physical RAM map:
  BIOS-e820: 0000000000000000 - 0000000000099800 (usable)
guest1 ~/LinuxScriptingBook/chapters/chap4 $
```

The next section shows file redirection.

Chapter 4 - Script 3

```
#!/bin/sh
#
# 5/8/2017
#
FN=/tmp/dmesg.txt
dmesg > $FN
echo "File $FN created."
exit 0
```

Try it on your system.

This shows how easy it is to create a script to perform commands that you would normally type on the command line. Also notice the use of the FN variable. If you want to use a different filename later, you only have to make the change in one place.

Subroutines

Now let's really get into subroutines. To do this we will use more of the tput commands:

```
tput cup <row><col>        # moves the cursor to row, col
tput cup 0 0               # cursor to the upper left hand side
```

```
tput cup $LINES $COLUMNS     # cursor to bottom right hand side
tput clear                   # clears the terminal screen
tput smso                    # bolds the text that follows
tput rmso                    # un-bolds the text that follows
```

Here is the script. This was mainly written to show the concept of a subroutine, however, it can also be used as a guide on writing interactive tools.

Chapter 4 - Script 4

```
#!/bin/sh
# 6/13/2017
# script4

# Subroutines
cls()
{
 tput clear
 return 0
}

home()
{
 tput cup 0 0
 return 0
}

end()
{
 let x=$COLUMNS-1
 tput cup $LINES $x
 echo -n "X"                 # no newline or else will scroll
}

bold()
{
 tput smso
```

```
}

unbold()
{
 tput rmso
}

underline()
{
 tput smul
}

normalline()
{
 tput rmul
}

# Code starts here
rc=0                            # return code
if [ $# -ne 1 ] ; then
 echo "Usage: script4 parameter"
 echo "Where parameter can be: "
 echo " home        - put an X at the home position"
 echo " cls         - clear the terminal screen"
 echo " end         - put an X at the last screen position"
 echo " bold        - bold the following output"
 echo " underline - underline the following output"
 exit 255
fi

parm=$1                         # main parameter 1

if [ "$parm" = "home" ] ; then
```

```
 echo "Calling subroutine home."
 home
 echo -n "X"
elif [ "$parm" = "cls" ] ; then
 cls
elif [ "$parm" = "end" ] ; then
 echo "Calling subroutine end."
 end
elif [ "$parm" = "bold" ] ; then
 echo "Calling subroutine bold."
 bold
 echo "After calling subroutine bold."
 unbold
 echo "After calling subroutine unbold."
elif [ "$parm" = "underline" ] ; then
 echo "Calling subroutine underline."
 underline
 echo "After subroutine underline."
 normalline
 echo "After subroutine normalline."
else
 echo "Unknown parameter: $parm"
 rc=1
fi

exit $rc
```

The following is the output:

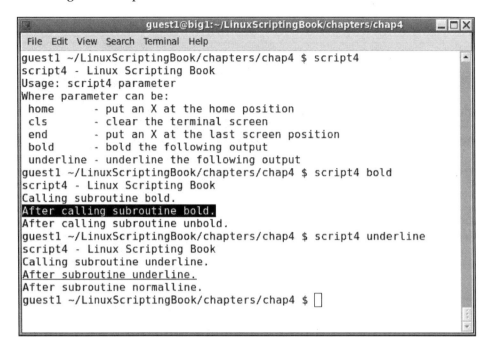

Try this on your system. If you run it with the `home` parameter it might look a little strange to you. The code puts a capital X at the `home  position` (0,0) and this causes the prompt to print one character over. Nothing is wrong here, it just looks a little weird. Don't worry if this still doesn't make sense to you, just go ahead and look at *Script 5*.

Using parameters

Okay, let's add some routines to this script to show how to use parameters with a `subroutine`. In order to make the output look better the `cls` routine is called first to clear the screen:

Chapter 4 - Script 5

```sh
#!/bin/sh

# 6/13/2017

# script5


# Subroutines
```

```
cls()
{
 tput clear
 return 0
}

home()
{
 tput cup 0 0
 return 0
}

end()
{
 let x=$COLUMNS-1
 tput cup $LINES $x
 echo -n "X"                        # no newline or else will scroll
}

bold()
{
 tput smso
}

unbold()
{
 tput rmso
}

underline()
{
 tput smul
}

normalline()
{
```

```
 tput rmul
}


move()                        # move cursor to row, col
{
 tput cup $1 $2
}


movestr()                     # move cursor to row, col
{
 tput cup $1 $2
 echo $3
}


# Code starts here
cls                           # clear the screen to make the output look
better
rc=0                          # return code
if [ $# -ne 1 ] ; then
  echo "Usage: script5 parameter"
  echo "Where parameter can be: "
  echo " home       - put an X at the home position"
  echo " cls        - clear the terminal screen"
  echo " end        - put an X at the last screen position"
  echo " bold       - bold the following output"
  echo " underline  - underline the following output"
  echo " move       - move cursor to row,col"
  echo " movestr    - move cursor to row,col and output string"
  exit 255
fi


parm=$1                       # main parameter 1


if [ "$parm" = "home" ] ; then
```

```
  home
  echo -n "X"
elif [ "$parm" = "cls" ] ; then
  cls
elif [ "$parm" = "end" ] ; then
  move 0 0
  echo "Calling subroutine end."
end
elif [ "$parm" = "bold" ] ; then
  echo "Calling subroutine bold."
  bold
  echo "After calling subroutine bold."
  unbold
  echo "After calling subroutine unbold."
elif [ "$parm" = "underline" ] ; then
  echo "Calling subroutine underline."
  underline
  echo "After subroutine underline."
  normalline
  echo "After subroutine normalline."
elif [ "$parm" = "move" ] ; then
  move 10 20
  echo "This line started at row 10 col 20"
elif [ "$parm" = "movestr" ] ; then
  movestr 15 40 "This line started at 15 40"
else
  echo "Unknown parameter: $parm"
  rc=1
fi

exit $rc
```

Since this script only has two extra functions you can just run them. This will be shown one command at a time as follows:

```
guest1 $ script5
```

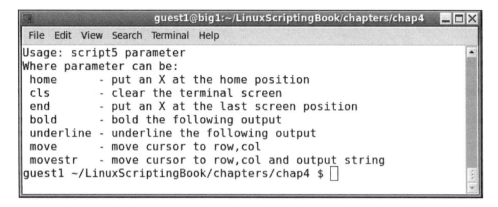

```
guest1 $ script5 move
```

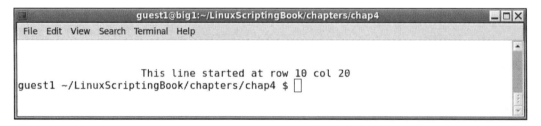

```
guest1 $ script5 movestr
```

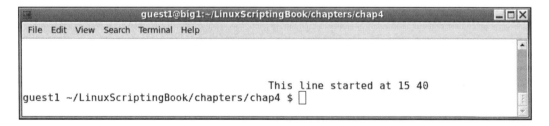

Since we are now placing the cursor at a specific location, the output should make more sense to you. Notice how the command-line prompt reappears where the last cursor position was.

You probably noticed that the parameters to a subroutine work just like with a script. Parameter 1 is $1, parameter 2 is $2, and so on. This is good and bad, good because you don't have to learn anything radically different. But bad in that it is very easy to get the $1, $2, vars mixed up if you are not careful.

A possible solution, and the one I use, is to assign the $1, $2, and so on variables in the main script to a variable with a good meaningful name.

For example, in these example scripts I set parm1 equal to $1 (parm1=$1), and so on.

Take a good look at the script in the next section:

Chapter 4 - Script 6

```sh
#!/bin/sh
#
# 6/13/2017
# script6

# Subroutines
sub1()
{
 echo "Entering sub1"
 rc1=0                       # default is no error
 if [ $# -ne 1 ] ; then
   echo "sub1 requires 1 parameter"
   rc1=1                     # set error condition
 else
   echo "1st parm: $1"
 fi

 echo "Leaving sub1"
 return $rc1                 # routine return code
}

sub2()
{
 echo "Entering sub2"
```

```
 rc2=0                           # default is no error
 if [ $# -ne 2 ] ; then
   echo "sub2 requires 2 parameters"
   rc2=1                         # set error condition
 else
   echo "1st parm: $1"
   echo "2nd parm: $2"
 fi
 echo "Leaving sub2"
 return $rc2                     # routine return code
}


sub3()
{
 echo "Entering sub3"
 rc3=0                           # default is no error
 if [ $# -ne 3 ] ; then
   echo "sub3 requires 3 parameters"
   rc3=1                         # set error condition
 else
   echo "1st parm: $1"
   echo "2nd parm: $2"
   echo "3rd parm: $3"
 fi
 echo "Leaving sub3"
 return $rc3                     # routine return code
}


cls()                           # clear screen
{
 tput clear
 return $?                       # return code from tput
}


causeanerror()
{
```

```
  echo "Entering causeanerror"
  tput firephasers
  return $?                         # return code from tput
}


# Code starts here
cls                                 # clear the screen
rc=$?
echo "return code from cls: $rc"
rc=0                                # reset the return code
if [ $# -ne 3 ] ; then
  echo "Usage: script6 parameter1 parameter2 parameter3"
  echo "Where all parameters are simple strings."
  exit 255
fi


parm1=$1                            # main parameter 1
parm2=$2                            # main parameter 2
parm3=$3                            # main parameter 3


# show main parameters
echo "parm1: $parm1   parm2: $parm2   parm3: $parm3"


sub1 "sub1-parm1"
echo "return code from sub1: $?"


sub2 "sub2-parm1"
echo "return code from sub2: $?"


sub3 $parm1 $parm2 $parm3
echo "return code from sub3: $?"


causeanerror
echo "return code from causeanerror: $?"


exit $rc
```

And here's the output

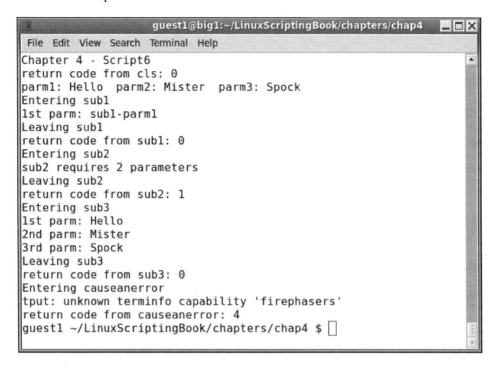

There are some new concepts here and so we will go through this one very carefully.

First, we define the subroutines. Notice that a return code has been added. A `cls` routine has also been included so that a return code could be shown.

We are now at the start of the code. The `cls` routine is called and then the return value from it is stored in the `rc` variable. Then the `echo` statement showing which script this is will be displayed.

So, why did I have to put the return code from the `cls` command into the `rc` var? Couldn't I have just displayed it after the `echo` of the script title? No, because the `echo $?` always refers to the command immediately preceding it. This is easy to forget so make sure you understand this point.

Okay, so now we reset the `rc` var to `0` and continue on. I could have used a different variable for this, but since the value of `rc` is not going to be needed again I chose to just reuse the `rc` variable.

Now, at the check for parameters, the `Usage` statement will be displayed if three parameters are not there.

After three parameters are entered we display them. This is always a good idea especially when first writing a script/program. You can always take it out later if it is not needed.

The first subroutine, sub1, is run with 1 parameter. This is checked and an error is displayed if needed.

The same thing happens with sub2, but in this case I intentionally set it to run with only one parameter so that the error message would be displayed.

For sub3, you can see that the main parameters are still accessible from a subroutine. In fact, all of the named variables are, and also the wildcard * and other file expansion tokens. Only the main script parameters cannot be accessed, which is why we put them into variables.

The final routine was created in order to show how errors can be handled. You can see that the tput command itself displayed the error, and then we also captured it in the script.

Finally, the script exits with the main rc variable.

As was mentioned earlier, this script has a lot in it so be sure to study it carefully. Note that when I wanted to show an error in tput, I just assumed that firephasers was going to be an unknown command. I would have been rather surprised if some phasers had actually shot out of (or worse, into) my computer!

Making a current backup of your work

And now, for another bonus the next section shows the script I used to backup my current book's chapter every 60 seconds:

Chapter 4 – Script 7

```sh
#!/bin/sh
#
# Auto backs up the file given if it has changed
# Assumes the cbS command exists
# Checks that ../back exists
# Copies to specific USB directory
```

```
# Checks if filename.bak exists on startup, copy if it doesn't

echo "autobackup by Lewis 5/9/2017 A"
if [ $# -ne 3 ] ; then
 echo "Usage: autobackup filename USB-backup-dir delay"
 exit 255
fi

# Create back directory if it does not exist
if [ ! -d back ] ; then
 mkdir back
fi

FN=$1                       # filename to monitor
USBdir=$2                   # USB directory to copy to
DELAY=$3                    # how often to check

if [ ! -f $FN ] ; then      # if no filename abort
 echo "File: $FN does not exist."
 exit 5
fi

if [ ! -f $FN.bak ] ; then
 cp $FN $FN.bak
fi

filechanged=0
while [ 1 ]
do
 cmp $FN $FN.bak
 rc=$?
 if [ $rc -ne 0 ] ; then
  cp $FN back
  cp $FN $USBdir
  cd back
```

```
    cbS $FN
    cd ..
    cp $FN $FN.bak
    filechanged=1
  fi


  sleep $DELAY
done
```

And for the output on my system

```
guest1@big1:~/LinuxScriptingBook/chapters/chap4                          _□×
 File  Edit  View  Search  Terminal  Help
guest1 ~/LinuxScriptingBook/chapters/chap4 $ script7 chapter4.txt /usb/bookbackup 60
autobackup by Lewis 5/9/2017 A
chapter4.txt chapter4.txt.bak differ: byte 37, line 4
cbS by Lewis 5/4/2017
File bak-4.chapter4.txt created.
chapter4.txt chapter4.txt.bak differ: byte 38, line 5
cbS by Lewis 5/4/2017
File bak-5.chapter4.txt created.
chapter4.txt chapter4.txt.bak differ: byte 38, line 5
cbS by Lewis 5/4/2017
File bak-6.chapter4.txt created.
chapter4.txt chapter4.txt.bak differ: byte 3304, line 86
cbS by Lewis 5/4/2017
File bak-7.chapter4.txt created.
```

There's not much in this script that we have not already covered. The informal comments at the top are mainly for me, so that I don't forget what I wrote or why.

The parms are checked and the back subdirectory is created if it does not already exist. I never seem to be able to remember to create it, so I let the script do it.

Next, the main variables are set up and then the .bak file is created if it doesn't exist (this helps with the logic).

In the while loop, which you can see runs forever, the cmp Linux command is used to see if the original file has changed from the backup file. If so, the cmp command returns non-zero and the file is copied back to the subdir as a numbered backup using our cbS script. The file is also copied to the backup directory, which in this case is my USB drive. The loop continues until I start a new chapter, in which case I press *Ctrl + C* to quit.

This is a good example of script automation, which will be covered in more detail in *Chapter 6, Automating Tasks with Scripts*.

Summary

We started with some very simple scripts and then proceeded to show some simple subroutines.

We then showed some subroutines that take parameters. Return codes were mentioned again to show how they work in subroutines. We including several scripts to show the concepts, and also included a special bonus script at no extra charge.

In the next chapter we will go over how to create interactive scripts.

Creating Interactive Scripts

5

This chapter shows how to read the keyboard in order to create interactive scripts.

The topics covered in this chapter are:

- How to use the `read` built-in command to query the keyboard.
- The different ways to use `read`.
- The use of traps (interrupts).

The reader will learn how to create interactive scripts.

The scripts we have looked at up to this point have run without much user interaction. The `read` command is used to create scripts that can query the keyboard. The code can then take action based on the input.

Here is a simple example:

Chapter 5 - Script 1

```
#!/bin/sh
#
# 5/16/2017
#
echo "script1 - Linux Scripting Book"

echo "Enter 'q' to quit."
rc=0
while [ $rc -eq 0 ]
do
 echo -n "Enter a string: "
```

```
 read str
 echo "str: $str"
 if [ "$str" = "q" ] ; then
  rc=1
 fi
done


echo "End of script1"
exit 0
```

And here is the output when run on my system:

This is a good one to run on your system. Try several different strings, numbers, and so on. Notice how the returned string contains whitespace, special characters, and so on. You don't have to quote anything, and if you do those will be returned as well.

You can also use the read command to put a simple pause into your script. This will allow you to see the output before it scrolls off the screen. It can also be used when debugging which will be shown in *Chapter 9*, *Debugging Scripts*.

The following script shows how to create a pause when the output gets to the last line of the screen:

Chapter 5 - Script 2

```
#!/bin/sh
#
# 5/16/2017
# Chapter 5 - Script 2
```

```
#
linecnt=1                    # line counter
loop=0                       # loop control var
while [ $loop -eq 0 ]
do
 echo "$linecnt  $RANDOM"    # display next random number
 let linecnt++
 if [ $linecnt -eq $LINES ] ; then
  linecnt=1
  echo -n "Press Enter to continue or q to quit: "
  read str                   # pause
  if [ "$str" = "q" ] ; then
   loop=1                     # end the loop
  fi
 fi
done

echo "End of script2"
exit 0
```

And here is the output when run on my system:

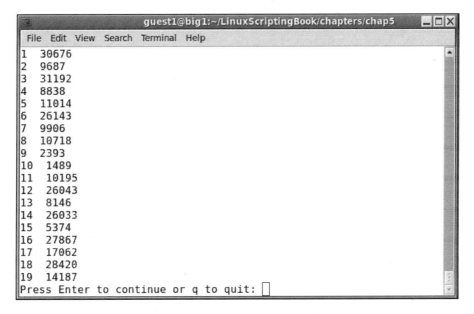

I pressed *Enter* twice, and then *Q* and *Enter* on the last one.

Let's try something a bit more interesting. This next script shows how to fill an array with values taken from the keyboard:

Chapter 5 - Script 3

```sh
#!/bin/sh
#
# 5/16/2017
#
echo "script3 - Linux Scripting Book"

if [ "$1" = "--help" ] ; then
 echo "Usage: script3"
 echo " Queries the user for values and puts them into an array."
 echo " Entering 'q' will halt the script."
 echo " Running 'script3 --help' shows this Usage message."
 exit 255
fi


x=0                          # subscript into array
loop=0                       # loop control variable
while [ $loop -eq 0 ]
do
  echo -n "Enter a value or q to quit: "
  read value
  if [ "$value" = "q" ] ; then
   loop=1
  else
   array[$x]="$value"
   let x++
  fi
done

let size=x
x=0
```

```
while [ $x -lt $size ]
do
 echo "array $x: ${array[x]}"
 let x++
done


echo "End of script3"
exit 0
```

And the output:

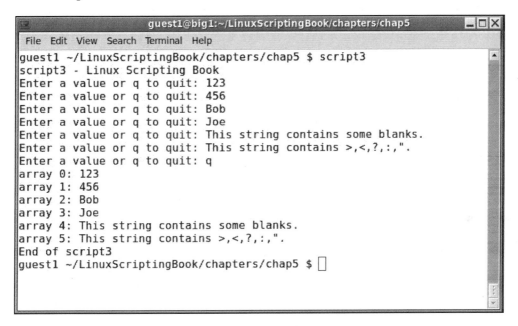

```
guest1@big1:~/LinuxScriptingBook/chapters/chap5
File  Edit  View  Search  Terminal  Help
guest1 ~/LinuxScriptingBook/chapters/chap5 $ script3
script3 - Linux Scripting Book
Enter a value or q to quit: 123
Enter a value or q to quit: 456
Enter a value or q to quit: Bob
Enter a value or q to quit: Joe
Enter a value or q to quit: This string contains some blanks.
Enter a value or q to quit: This string contains >,<,?,:,".
Enter a value or q to quit: q
array 0: 123
array 1: 456
array 2: Bob
array 3: Joe
array 4: This string contains some blanks.
array 5: This string contains >,<,?,:,".
End of script3
guest1 ~/LinuxScriptingBook/chapters/chap5 $ 
```

Since this script does not require any parameters I decided to add a Usage statement. This will display if the user runs it with --help and is a common feature in many system scripts and programs.

The only thing new in this script is the read command. The loop and array variables were discussed in an earlier chapter. Note again that, with the read command what you type is what you get.

Now let's create a complete interactive script. But first we need to check the size of the current terminal. If it is too small, the output of your script may become garbled and the user may not know why or how to fix it.

The following script contains a subroutine that checks the size of the terminal:

Chapter 5 - Script 4

```
#!/bin/sh
#
# 5/16/2017
#
echo "script4 - Linux Scripting Book"

checktermsize()
{
 rc1=0                          # default is no error
 if [[ $LINES -lt $1 || $COLUMNS -lt $2 ]] ; then
  rc1=1                         # set return code
 fi
 return $rc1
}

rc=0                            # default is no error
checktermsize 40 90             # check terminal size
rc=$?
if [ $rc -ne 0 ] ; then
  echo "Return code: $rc from checktermsize"
fi

exit $rc
```

Run this on your system with different-sized terminals to check the result. As you can see from the code, it's okay if the terminal is larger than needed; it just can't be too small.

A word about terminal sizes: When using the `tput` cursor movement commands remember that it is row then column. However, most modern GUIs go by column then row. This is unfortunate as it is very easy to get them mixed up.

Now let's look at a full interactive script:

Chapter 5 - Script 5

```
#!/bin/sh
#
# 5/27/2017
#
echo "script5 - Linux Scripting Book"


# Subroutines
cls()
{
 tput clear
}


move()                          # move cursor to row, col
{
 tput cup $1 $2
}


movestr()                       # move cursor to row, col
{
 tput cup $1 $2
 echo -n "$3"                   # display string
}


checktermsize()
{
 rc1=0                          # default is no error
 if [[ $LINES -lt $1 || $COLUMNS -lt $2 ]] ; then
  rc1=1                         # set return code
```

```
 fi
 return $rc1
}


init()                          # set up the cursor position array
{
 srow[0]=2;   scol[0]=7         # name
 srow[1]=4;   scol[1]=12        # address 1
 srow[2]=6;   scol[2]=12        # address 2
 srow[3]=8;   scol[3]=7         # city
 srow[4]=8;   scol[4]=37        # state
 srow[5]=8;   scol[5]=52        # zip code
 srow[6]=10;  scol[6]=8         # email
}


drawscreen()                    # main screen draw routine
{
 cls                            # clear the screen
 movestr 0 25 "Chapter 5 - Script 5"
 movestr 2 1 "Name:"
 movestr 4 1 "Address 1:"
 movestr 6 1 "Address 2:"
 movestr 8 1 "City:"
 movestr 8 30 "State:"
 movestr 8 42 "Zip code:"
 movestr 10 1 "Email:"
}


getdata()
{
 x=0                            # array subscript
 rc1=0                          # loop control variable
 while [ $rc1 -eq 0 ]
 do
  row=${srow[x]}; col=${scol[x]}
  move $row $col
```

```
   read array[x]
   let x++
   if [ $x -eq $sizeofarray ] ; then
    rc1=1
   fi
 done
 return 0
}


showdata()
{
 fn=0
 echo ""
 read -p "Enter filename, or just Enter to skip: " filename
 if [ -n "$filename" ] ; then         # if not blank
  echo "Writing to '$filename'"
 fn=1                     # a filename was given
 fi
 echo ""                  # skip 1 line
 echo "Data array contents: "
 y=0
 while [ $y -lt $sizeofarray ]
 do
  echo "$y - ${array[$y]}"
  if [ $fn -eq 1 ] ; then
   echo "$y - ${array[$y]}">>"$filename"
  fi
  let y++
 done
 return 0
}


# Code starts here
sizeofarray=7                 # number of array elements

if [ "$1" = "--help" ] ; then
```

```
echo "Usage: script5 --help"
echo " This script shows how to create an interactive screen program."
exit 255
fi

checktermsize 25 80
rc=$?
if [ $rc -ne 0 ] ; then
echo "Please size the terminal to 25x80 and try again."
exit 1
fi

init                        # initialize the screen array
drawscreen                  # draw the screen
getdata                     # cursor movement and data input routine
showdata                    # display the data

exit 0
```

Here is some example output:

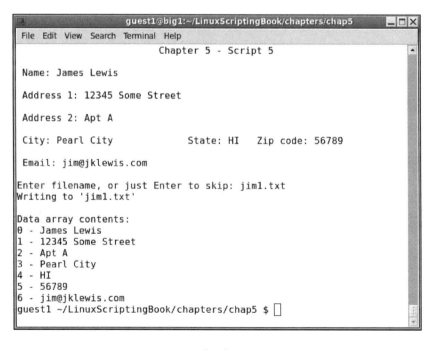

There is a lot of new information here, so let's take a look. First the subroutines are defined, and you can see we included the `checktermsize` subroutine from the preceding *Script 4*.

The `init` routine sets up the cursor placement array. It's good programming practice to put initial values in a subroutine, particularly if it is going to be called again.

The `drawscreen` routine displays the initial form. Note that I could have used the values in the `srow` and `scol` array here, however, I didn't want the script to look too cluttered.

Look very carefully at the `getdata` routine because this is where the fun begins:

- First the array subscript x and control var `rc1` are set to `0`.
- In the loop the cursor is placed at the first position (`Name:`).
- The keyboard is queried and the user's input goes into the array at sub x.
- x is incremented and we go to the next field.
- If x is equal to the size of the array we leave the loop. Keep in mind that we start counting at `0`.

The `showdata` routine displays the array data and then we are done.

[Note that if the script is run with the `--help` option the `Usage` message is displayed.]

This is just a small example of an interactive script to show the basic concepts. In a later chapter we will go into this in more detail.

The `read` command can be used in a number of different ways. Here are a few examples:

```
read var
```

Wait for input of characters into the variable var.

```
read -p "string" var
```

Display contents of string, stay on the line, and wait for input.

```
read -p "Enter password:" -s var
```

Display "Enter password:", but do not echo the typing of the input. Note that a carriage return is not output after Enter is pressed.

```
read -n 1 var
```

The -n option means to wait for that number of characters and then continue, it does not wait for an *Enter* press.

In this example it will wait for 1 char and then go. This can be useful in utility scripts and games:

Chapter 5 - Script 6

```
#!/bin/sh
#
# 5/27/2017
#
echo "Chapter 5 - Script 6"

rc=0                       # return code
while [ $rc -eq 0 ]
do
 read -p "Enter value or q to quit: " var
 echo "var: $var"
 if [ "$var" = "q" ] ; then
  rc=1
 fi
done

rc=0                       # return code
while [ $rc -eq 0 ]
do
 read -p "Password: " -s var
 echo ""                   # carriage return
 echo "var: $var"
if [ "$var" = "q" ] ; then
  rc=1
 fi
done

echo "Press some keys and q to quit."
```

```
rc=0                          # return code
while [ $rc -eq 0 ]
do
 read -n 1 -s var             # wait for 1 char, does not output it
 echo $var                    # output it here
 if [ "$var" = "q" ] ; then
  rc=1
 fi
done


exit $rc
```

And the output:

```
guest1@big1:~/LinuxScriptingBook/chapters/chap5
File  Edit  View  Search  Terminal  Help
guest1 ~/LinuxScriptingBook/chapters/chap5 $ script6
Chapter 5 - Script 6
Enter value or q to quit: Hello There
var: Hello There
Enter value or q to quit: Linux Rules
var: Linux Rules
Enter value or q to quit: q
var: q
Password:
var: thisisapassword
Password:
var: q
Press some keys and q to quit.
1
3
5
7
y
j
i
l
q
guest1 ~/LinuxScriptingBook/chapters/chap5 $
```

The comments in the script should make this one pretty self explanatory. The read command has a few more options, one of which will be shown in the next script.

Another way to query the keyboard is by using what is called a trap. This is a subroutine that is accessed when a special key sequence is pressed, such as *Ctrl + C.*

Here is an example of using a trap:

Chapter 5 - Script 7

```
#!/bin/sh
#
# 5/16/2017
#
echo "script7 - Linux Scripting Book"

trap catchCtrlC INT          # Initialize the trap


# Subroutines
catchCtrlC()
{
 echo "Entering catchCtrlC routine."
}


# Code starts here

echo "Press Ctrl-C to trigger the trap, 'Q' to exit."

loop=0
while [ $loop -eq 0 ]
do
 read -t 1 -n 1 str          # wait 1 sec for input or for 1 char
 rc=$?

 if [ $rc -gt 128 ] ; then
  echo "Timeout exceeded."
 fi

 if [ "$str" = "Q" ] ; then
  echo "Exiting the script."
```

```
  loop=1
 fi


done


exit 0
```

Here is the output on my system:

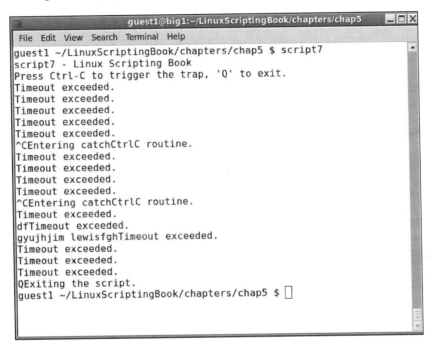

Try running this one on your system. Press some keys and see the response. Press *Ctrl + C* a few times as well. When done press *Q*.

That `read` statement needs some further explanation. Using `read` with the `-t` option (timeout) means to wait that many seconds for a character. If one is not input in the allotted time it will return a code with a value greater than 128. As we have seen before, the `-n 1` option tells `read` to wait for 1 character. So this means we are waiting 1 second for 1 character. This is another way `read` can be used to create a game or other interactive script.

Using a trap is a good way to catch an accidental press of *Ctrl + C* which could cause data to be lost. One word of caution however, if you do decide to catch *Ctrl + C* make sure your script has some other way to exit. In the simple script above the user must type a *Q* to exit.

If you get yourself into a situation where you can't exit a script you can use the `kill` command.

For example, if I had needed to stop `script7` the directions would be follows:

```
guest1 $ ps auxw | grep script7
guest1    17813   0.0  0.0 106112   1252 pts/32   S+    17:23    0:00 /bin/sh
./script7
guest1    17900   0.0  0.0 103316    864 pts/18   S+    17:23    0:00 grep
script7
guest1    29880   0.0  0.0  10752   1148 pts/17   S+    16:47    0:00 kw
script7
guest1 $ kill -9 17813
guest1 $
```

In the terminal where `script7` was running you will see it has stopped with the word `Killed` in it.

Note, be sure to kill the right process!

In the example above, PID `29880` is my text editor session where I am writing `script7`. Killing that would not be a good idea :).

Now for some fun! The next script allows you to draw crude pictures on the screen:

Chapter 5 - Script 8

```
#!/bin/sh
#
# 5/16/2017
#
echo "script8 - Linux Scripting Book"

# Subroutines
cls()
{
```

```
  tput clear
}


move()                        # move cursor to row, col
{
  tput cup $1 $2
}


movestr()                     # move cursor to row, col
{
  tput cup $1 $2
  echo -n "$3"                # display string
}


init()                        # set initial values
{
  minrow=1                    # terminal boundaries
  maxrow=24
  mincol=0
  maxcol=79
  startrow=1
  startcol=0
}


restart()                     # clears screen, sets initial cursor
position
{
  cls
  movestr 0 0 "Arrow keys move cursor. 'x' to draw, 'd' to erase, '+' to
restart, 'Q' to quit."
  row=$startrow
  col=$startcol

  draw=0                      # default is not drawing
  drawchar=""
}
```

```
checktermsize2()                  # must be the specified size
{
 rc1=0                            # default is no error
 if [[ $LINES -ne $1 || $COLUMNS -ne $2 ]] ; then
  rc1=1                           # set return code
 fi
 return $rc1
}


# Code starts here
if [ "$1" = "--help" ] ; then
 echo "Usage: script7 --help"
 echo " This script shows the basics on how to create a game."
 echo " Use the arrow keys to move the cursor."
 echo " Press c to restart and Q to quit."
 exit 255
fi


checktermsize2 25 80            # terminal must be this size
rc=$?
if [ $rc -ne 0 ] ; then
 echo "Please size the terminal to 25x80 and try again."
 exit 1
fi


init                           # initialize values
restart                        # set starting cursor pos and clear screen

loop=1
while [ $loop -eq 1 ]
do
 move $row $col                # position the cursor here
 read -n 1 -s ch

 case "$ch" in
```

```
A) if [ $row -gt $minrow ] ; then
      let row--
   fi
   ;;
B) if [ $row -lt $maxrow ] ; then
      let row++
   fi
   ;;
C) if [ $col -lt $maxcol ] ; then
      let col++
   fi
   ;;
D) if [ $col -gt $mincol ] ; then
      let col--
   fi
   ;;
d) echo -n ""              # delete char
   ;;
x) if [ $col -lt $maxcol ] ; then
      echo -n "X"          # put char
      let col++
   fi
   ;;
 +) restart ;;
 Q) loop=0 ;;
 esac
done

movestr 24 0 "Script completed normally."
echo ""                    # carriage return

exit 0
```

This was fun to write and a bit more fun to play with than I expected it to be.

One thing we haven't covered yet is the `case` statement. This is similar to an `if...then...else` but makes the code easier to read. Basically, the value that was input to the `read` statement is checked for a match in each `case` clause. If it matches, that stanza is executed and then control goes to the line after the `esac` statement. It also does this if there is no match.

Try this script, and remember to make the terminal 25x80 (or 80x25 if that is how your GUI works).

Here is just one example of what can be done with this script:

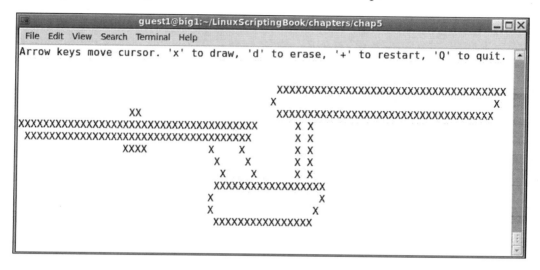

Well okay I guess this shows that I am not much of an artist. I will stick to programming and writing books.

Summary

In this chapter we showed how to use the `read` built-in command to query the keyboard. We explained some of the different options to read and also covered the use of traps. A simple drawing game was also included.

The next chapter will show how to automate a script so that it can run unattended. We will explain how `cron` can be used to run the script at a specific time. The archival programs `zip` and `tar` will also be covered as they are very useful when creating automated back up scripts.

6

Automating Tasks with Scripts

This chapter shows how to automate various tasks using scripts.

The topics covered in this chapter are as follows:

- How to create a script to automate a task.
- The proper way to use cron to run the script automatically at specific times.
- How to use ZIP and TAR to perform compressed backups.
- Source code examples.

The reader will learn how to create automated scripts.

We talked about the `sleep` command in *Chapter 3, Using Loops and the sleep Command*. It can be used to create an automated script (that is, one that runs at a specific time with no user intervention) as long as a few guidelines are followed.

This very simple script will reinforce what we covered in *Chapter 3 Using Loops and the sleep Command* about using the `sleep` command for automation:

Chapter 6 - Script 1

```
#!/bin/sh
#
# 5/23/2017
#
echo "script1 - Linux Scripting Book"
while [ true ]
```

```
do
   date
   sleep 1d
done
echo "End of script1"
exit 0
```

If you run this on your system and wait a few days you will start to see the date slip a little. This is because the sleep command inserts a delay into the script, it does not mean that it is going to run the script at the same time every day.

 The following script shows this problem in a bit more detail. Note that this is an example of what not to do.

Chapter 6 - Script 2

```
#!/bin/sh
#
# 5/23/2017
#
echo "script2 - Linux Scripting Book"
while [ true ]
do
  # Run at 3 am
  date | grep -q 03:00:
  rc=$?
  if [ $rc -eq 0 ] ; then
   echo "Run commands here."
   date
  fi
  sleep 60                    # sleep 60 seconds
done
echo "End of script2"
exit 0
```

The first thing you will notice is that this script will run until it is either manually terminated with *Ctrl + C* or the kill command (or when the machine goes down for whatever reason). It is common for automated scripts to just run forever.

The `date` command, as run without any parameters, returns something like this:

```
guest1 $ date
Fri May 19 15:11:54 HST 2017
```

So now all we have to do is use `grep` to match that time. Unfortunately, there is a very subtle problem here. It has been verified that it is possible for this to miss from time to time. For example, if the time has just changed to 3:00 am and the program is now in the sleep it might already be 3:01 when it wakes up. In my early days in computing I had seen code like this all the time in my jobs and never gave it a single thought. When some important backups were missed one day my team was asked to figure out what was going on and we discovered this issue. A quick fix for this would be to change the seconds to 59, however, a better way is to use cron which will be shown later in this chapter.

Notice the `-q` option to `grep`, this simply tells it to suppress any output. Feel free to take this out if you want, especially when first writing the script. Also notice that `grep` returns `0` when a match is found, non-zero otherwise.

With all this said let's look at some simple automated scripts. I have been running the following on my Linux systems since 1996:

Chapter 6 - Script 3

```
#!/bin/sh
#
# 5/23/2017
#
echo "script3 - Linux Scripting Book"
FN=/tmp/log1.txt              # log file
while [ true ]
do
   echo Pinging $PROVIDER
   ping -c 1 $PROVIDER
   rc=$?
   if [ $rc -ne 0 ] ; then
     echo Cannot ping $PROVIDER
     date >> $FN
     echo Cannot ping $PROVIDER >> $FN
   fi
```

```
    sleep 60
done
echo "End of script3"          # 60 seconds
exit 0
```

And the output on my system:

```
guest1@big1:~/LinuxScriptingBook/chapters/chap6

File  Edit  View  Search  Terminal  Help

guest1 ~/LinuxScriptingBook/chapters/chap6 $ script3
script3 - Linux Scripting Book
Pinging twc.com
PING twc.com (71.74.183.9) 56(84) bytes of data.
64 bytes from 71.74.183.9: icmp_seq=1 ttl=50 time=119 ms

--- twc.com ping statistics ---
1 packets transmitted, 1 received, 0% packet loss, time 128ms
rtt min/avg/max/mdev = 119.551/119.551/119.551/0.000 ms
Pinging twc.com
PING twc.com (71.74.183.9) 56(84) bytes of data.
64 bytes from 71.74.183.9: icmp_seq=1 ttl=50 time=119 ms

--- twc.com ping statistics ---
1 packets transmitted, 1 received, 0% packet loss, time 248ms
rtt min/avg/max/mdev = 119.106/119.106/119.106/0.000 ms
Pinging twc.com
PING twc.com (71.74.183.9) 56(84) bytes of data.
64 bytes from 71.74.183.9: icmp_seq=1 ttl=50 time=119 ms

--- twc.com ping statistics ---
1 packets transmitted, 1 received, 0% packet loss, time 211ms
rtt min/avg/max/mdev = 119.979/119.979/119.979/0.000 ms
Pinging twc.com
PING twc.com (71.74.183.9) 56(84) bytes of data.
64 bytes from 71.74.183.9: icmp_seq=1 ttl=50 time=120 ms
^C

guest1 ~/LinuxScriptingBook/chapters/chap6 $
```

I ran it just three times, however, it would go forever. Before running this on your system let's talk about that PROVIDER environment variable. I have several scripts on my system that deal with the Internet and I found myself constantly changing providers. It didn't take too long to realize that this was a great time to use an env var, hence PROVIDER.

This is in my /root/.bashrc and /home/guest1/.bashrc files:

```
export PROVIDER=twc.com
```

Substitute yours as needed. Notice too that when a failure occurs it is being written to the screen and to a file. Since the `>>` append operator is being used the file might eventually get rather large so plan accordingly if your connection is not very stable.

 Be careful they you do not ping or otherwise access a company site too many times in a short time frame. This could be detected and your access might be denied.

Here is a script that detects when a user has either logged on or off your system:

Chapter 6 - Script 4

```sh
#!/bin/sh
#
# 5/23/2017
#
echo "Chapter 6 - Script 4"
numusers=`who | wc -l`
while [ true ]
do
   currusers=`who | wc -l`          # get current number of users
   if [ $currusers -gt $numusers ] ; then
     echo "Someone new has logged on!!!!!!!!!!!!"
     date
     who
#    beep
     numusers=$currusers
   elif [ $currusers -lt $numusers ] ; then
     echo "Someone logged off."
     date
     numusers=$currusers
   fi
   sleep 1                 # sleep 1 second
done
```

Here's the output (adjusted for length):

```
guest1@big1:~/LinuxScriptingBook/chapters/chap6              _□X
File  Edit  View  Search  Terminal  Help
guest1 ~/LinuxScriptingBook/chapters/chap6 $ script4
Chapter 6 - Script 4
Someone new has logged on!!!!!!!!!!!!
Sat May 27 17:45:14 HST 2017
guest1   tty1           2017-01-12 16:05
guest1   pts/0          2017-01-12 16:13 (:0.0)
root     pts/1          2017-01-12 16:14 (:0.0)
root     pts/2          2017-01-12 16:14 (:0.0)
root     pts/3          2017-01-12 16:14 (:0.0)
root     pts/4          2017-01-12 16:14 (:0.0)
guest1   pts/5          2017-01-12 21:56 (:0.0)
guest1   pts/6          2017-01-15 14:01 (:0.0)
guest1   pts/7          2017-01-15 14:17 (:0.0)
guest1   pts/8          2017-01-17 20:12 (:0.0)
guest1   pts/9          2017-02-10 13:29 (:0.0)
guest1   pts/10         2017-01-12 16:21 (:0.0)
Someone logged off.
Sat May 27 17:45:31 HST 2017

guest1 ~/LinuxScriptingBook/chapters/chap6 $ □
```

This script checks the output from the who command to see if it has changed since the last run. If so it takes the appropriate action. If you have a beep command or equivalent on your system this is a good place to use it.

Take a look at this statement:

```
currusers=`who | wc -l`            # get current number of users
```

This needs some clarification as we have not covered it yet. Those back-tick characters mean to run the command(s) inside and put the result into the variable. In this case, the who command is piped into the wc -l command to count the number of lines. This value is then put into the currusers variable. If this sounds a bit complicated don't worry, it will be covered in greater detail in the next chapter.

The remainder of the script should already be clear as we have covered this before. If you decide to run something like this on your system just remember that it will trigger every time a new terminal is opened.

Cron

Okay, now for some real fun. If you have been using Linux for even just a short amount of time you are probably already aware of cron. This is a daemon, or background process, that executes commands at specific times.

Cron reads a file called `crontab` once a minute to determine if a command needs to be run.

For the examples in this chapter we will focus on the `crontab` for a guest account only (not for root).

Using my `guest1` account here is what it would look like the first time it is run. It would be a good idea to follow along on your system under a guest account:

```
guest1 $ crontab -l
no crontab for guest1
guest1 $
```

That makes sense as we have not created a `crontab` file for `guest1` yet. It is not meant to be edited directly and so the `crontab -e` command is used.

Run `crontab -e` under a guest account on your system now.

Here is a screenshot of how it appears on my system when using vi:

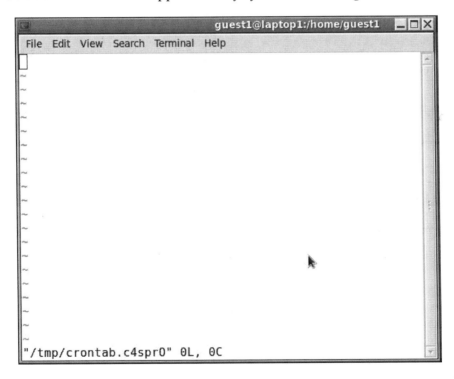

As you can see the `crontab` command creates a temporary file. It is unfortunate that this file comes up empty as they should have provided a template. Let's add one now. Copy and paste the following text into the file:

```
# this is the crontab file for guest1
# min   hour    day of month  month  day of week       command
# 0-59  0-23    1-31          1-12   0-6
#                                    Sun=0 Mon=1 Tue=2 Wed=3 Thu=4 Fri=5
Sat=6
```

Substitute `guest1` for your user name. This now gives us an idea of what goes where.

To this file add the following line:

```
  *       *       *       *       *             date > /dev/pts/31
```

The * means to match everything in the field. So in essence this line will fire once a minute.

We are using the redirection operator to write the output from the `echo` command to another terminal. Substitute yours as appropriate.

Try the above on your system. Remember you must save the file first, and you should see this output:

```
guest1 $ crontab -e
crontab: installing new crontab
guest1 $
```

This means the addition was successful. Now wait for the next minute to come around. You should see the current date show up in the other terminal.

We can now see the basics of cron. Here are a few quick pointers:

```
0   0   *   *   *   command       # run every day at midnight
0   3   *   *   *   command       # run every day at 3 am
30  9   1   *   *   command       # run at 9:30 am on the first of
the month
45  14  *   *   0   command       # run at 2:45 pm on Sundays
0   0   25  12  *   command       # run at midnight on my birthday
```

This is just a very small subset of how the date and times can be set in cron. For more information consult the `man` pages for cron and `crontab`.

One thing that needs to be mentioned is the PATH for a user's cron. It does not source the user's .bashrc file. You can verify this by adding the following line:

```
*    *    *    *    *    echo $PATH > /dev/pts/31    # check the PATH
```

On my CentOS 6.8 system it shows:

```
/usr/bin:/bin
```

To get around this problem you can source your .bashrc file:

```
*    *    *    *    *    source $HOME/.bashrc;  echo $PATH > /dev/pts/31
# check the PATH
```

This should now show the real path. The EDITOR env var was mentioned in *Chapter 2, Working with Variables*. If you want crontab to use a different text editor you can set EDITOR to the path/name of the one you want.

For example, on my system I have this:

```
export EDITOR=/home/guest1/bin/kw
```

So when I run crontab -e I get this:

```
 guest1@big1:~/LinuxScriptingBook                                    _ □ X
 File  Edit  View  Search  Terminal  Help
    ---- Top of file ----
# this is the crontab file for guest1

# min    hour    day of month   month   day of week        command
# 0-59   0-23      1-31          1-12    0-6  Sun=0
#                                        Sun=0 Mon=1 Tue=2 Wed=3 Thu=4 Fri=5 Sat=6

TTY=/dev/pts/31

*  *  *  *  *  source $HOME/.bashrc; echo $PATH > $TTY

 0  18  *  *  4  /home/guest1/bin/which-can    # Thursday at 6 pm


    ---- Bottom of file ----




                                                    big1       Mon May 22  2:59pm ===
                                                    Line     9  Col    1 NEW         13
Lewis Linux Editor 5/5/2017    /tmp/crontab.7pfqyD
```

Another thing that should be mentioned is if you make a mistake when using `crontab` in some cases it will tell you when you attempt to save the file. But it cannot check everything so be careful. Also, if a command gets an error `crontab` will use the mail system to notify the user. So, with this in mind you may need to run the `mail` command from time to time when using cron.

Now that we have looked at the basics let's create a backup script that uses the `zip` command. If you are not familiar with `zip` don't worry, this will get you up to speed quickly. On a Linux system most people just use the `tar` command, however, if you know how `zip` works you can share files with Windows users more easily.

In a directory under a guest account run these commands on your system. As usual I used `/home/guest1/LinuxScriptingBook`:

Make a `work` directory:

```
guest1 ~/LinuxScriptingBook $ mkdir work
```

Change to it:

```
guest1 ~/LinuxScriptingBook $ cd work
```

Create some temporary files, and/or copy a few existing files to this directory:

```
guest1 ~/LinuxScriptingBook/work $ route > route.txt
guest1 ~/LinuxScriptingBook/work $ ifconfig > ifconfig.txt
guest1 ~/LinuxScriptingBook/work $ ls -la /usr > usr.txt
guest1 ~/LinuxScriptingBook/work $ cp /etc/motd .
```

Get a listing:

```
guest1 ~/LinuxScriptingBook/work $ ls -la
total 24
drwxrwxr-x 2 guest1 guest1 4096 May 23 09:44 .
drwxr-xr-x 8 guest1 guest1 4096 May 22 15:18 ..
-rw-rw-r-- 1 guest1 guest1 1732 May 23 09:44 ifconfig.txt
-rw-r--r-- 1 guest1 guest1 1227 May 23 09:44 motd
-rw-rw-r-- 1 guest1 guest1  335 May 23 09:44 route.txt
-rw-rw-r-- 1 guest1 guest1  724 May 23 09:44 usr.txt
```

Zip them up:

```
guest1 ~/LinuxScriptingBook/work $ zip work1.zip *
  adding: ifconfig.txt (deflated 69%)
  adding: motd (deflated 49%)
  adding: route.txt (deflated 52%)
  adding: usr.txt (deflated 66%)
```

Get another listing:

```
guest1 ~/LinuxScriptingBook/work $ ls -la
total 28
drwxrwxr-x 2 guest1 guest1 4096 May 23 09:45 .
drwxr-xr-x 8 guest1 guest1 4096 May 22 15:18 ..
-rw-rw-r-- 1 guest1 guest1 1732 May 23 09:44 ifconfig.txt
-rw-r--r-- 1 guest1 guest1 1227 May 23 09:44 motd
-rw-rw-r-- 1 guest1 guest1  335 May 23 09:44 route.txt
-rw-rw-r-- 1 guest1 guest1  724 May 23 09:44 usr.txt
-rw-rw-r-- 1 guest1 guest1 2172 May 23 09:45 work1.zip
```

There is now file `work1.zip` in that directory. The syntax to create a `zip` file is:

```
zip [optional parameters] filename.zip list-of-files-to-include
```

To unzip it:

```
unzip filename.zip
```

To view (or list) the contents of a `zip` file without extracting it:

```
unzip -l filename.zip
```

This is also a good way to ensure that the `.zip` file was created properly, because unzip will report an error if it cannot read the file. Note that the `zip` command not only creates a `.zip` file but it also compresses the data. This makes for smaller backup files.

Here's a short script that uses `zip` to back up some files:

Chapter 6 - Script 5

```
#!/bin/sh
#
# 5/23/2017
#
echo "script5 - Linux Scripting Book"
FN=work1.zip
cd /tmp
mkdir work 2> /dev/null        # suppress message if directory already exists
cd work
cp /etc/motd .
cp /etc/issue .
ls -la /tmp > tmp.txt
ls -la /usr > usr.txt
rm $FN 2> /dev/null            # remove any previous file
zip $FN *
echo File "$FN" created.
# cp to an external drive, and/or scp to another computer
echo "End of script5"
exit 0
```

And the output on my system:

```
guest1@big1:~/LinuxScriptingBook/chapters/chap6
 File  Edit  View  Search  Terminal  Help
guest1 ~/LinuxScriptingBook/chapters/chap6 $ script5
script5 - Linux Scripting Book
  adding: issue (stored 0%)
  adding: motd (deflated 49%)
  adding: tmp.txt (deflated 66%)
  adding: usr.txt (deflated 66%)
File work1.zip created.
End of script5
guest1 ~/LinuxScriptingBook/chapters/chap6 $
```

This is a really simple script, however it shows the basics of using the `zip` command to backup some files.

Suppose we wanted to run this every day at midnight. Assuming `script5` was located under `/tmp`, the `crontab` entry would be the following:

```
guest1 /tmp/work $ crontab -l
# this is the crontab file for guest1


# min    hour    day of month  month   day of week        command
# 0-59   0-23    1-31          1-12    0-6   Sun=0
#                                      Sun=0 Mon=1 Tue=2 Wed=3 Thu=4 Fri=5
Sat=6


0 0 * * * /tmp/script5
```

In this case we did not have to source the `/home/guest1/.bashrc` file. Also notice that any errors get sent to the User's mail account. The zip command can do a whole lot more than just this, for example it can recurse into directories. For more information consult the man pages.

Now let's talk about the Linux `tar` command. It is used more frequently than the `zip` command and is better at getting all files, even hidden ones. Referring back to the `/tmp/work directory`, here is how you would use `tar` to back it up. It is assumed the files are still there from the previous script:

```
guest1 /tmp $ tar cvzf work1.gz work/
work/
work/motd
work/tmp.txt
work/issue
work/work1.zip
work/usr.txt
guest1 /tmp $
```

There is now file `work1.gz` under the `/tmp` directory. It is a compressed archive of the contents of all the files under `/tmp/work`, including the `.zip` file we created earlier.

The syntax for tar is a little cryptic at first but you will get used to it. Some of the features available in tar are:

Parameter	Feature
c	create an archive
x	extract an archive
v	use the verbose option
z	use gunzip style compression (.gz)
f	the filename to create/extract

Note that if you do not include the z option the file will not be compressed. By convention the file extension would then just be tar. Note that the user controls the actual name of the file, not the tar command.

Okay so now we have a compressed tar-gz file (or archive). Here is how to un-compress and extract the files. We will do this under /home/guest1:

```
guest1 /home/guest1 $ tar xvzf /tmp/work1.gz
work/
work/motd
work/tmp.txt
work/issue
work/work1.zip
work/usr.txt
guest1 /home/guest1 $
```

Using tar to backup a system is really convenient. It's also a great way to configure a new machine with your personal files. For example, I routinely back up the following directories on my primary system:

```
/home/guest1
/lewis
/temp
/root
```

These files are then auto-copied to an external USB drive. Remember that tar automatically recurses into directories and also gets every file, including hidden ones. Tar also has many other options that control how the archive is created. One of the most common options is to exclude certain directories.

For example, when backing up /home/guest1 there is really no reason to include the .cache, Cache, .thumbnails, and so on directories.

The option to exclude directories is `--exclude=<directory name>` and that is shown in the next script.

Here are the backup programs that I use on my primary Linux system. It is two scripts, one to schedule the backup and one to actually perform the work. I mainly did this so that I could make changes to the actual backup script without turning off the scheduler script. The first thing that needs to be set up is the `crontab` entry. Here is what it looks like on my system:

```
guest1 $ crontab -l
# this is the crontab file for guest1
# min    hour    day of month   month   day of week       command
# 0-59   0-23    1-31           1-12    0-6  Sun=0
#                                       Sun=0 Mon=1 Tue=2 Wed=3 Thu=4 Fri=5
Sat=6
TTY=/dev/pts/31


  0   3   *   *   *   touch /tmp/runbackup-cron.txt
```

This will create the file `/tmp/backup-cron.txt` at approximately 3 am every day.

Note that the following scripts must be run as root:

Chapter 6 - Script 6

```
#!/bin/sh
#
# runbackup1 - this version watches for file from crontab
#
# 6/3/2017 - mainlogs now under /data/mainlogs
#
VER="runbackup1 6/4/2017 A"
FN=/tmp/runbackup-cron.txt
DR=/wd1                      # symbolic link to external drive


tput clear
echo $VER


# Insure backup drive is mounted
```

```
file $DR | grep broken
rc=$?
if [ $rc -eq 0  ] ; then
 echo "ERROR: USB drive $DR is not mounted!!!!!!!!!!!!!!"
 beep
 exit 255
fi


cd $LDIR/backup

while [ true ]
do
 # crontab creates the file at 3 am

 if [ -f $FN ] ; then
  rm $FN
  echo Running backup1 ...
  backup1 | tee /data/mainlogs/mainlog`date '+%Y%m%d'`.txt
  echo $VER
 fi


 sleep 60                      # check every minute
done
```

There's a lot of information here so we will go through it line by line:

- The script first sets up the variables, clears the screen, and displays the name of the script.
- The DR variable is assigned to my USB external drive (wd1) which is a symbolic link.
- A check is then performed using the file command to ensure that /wd1 has been mounted. If it has not, the file command will return broken symbolic link, grep will trigger on this, and the script will abort.
- If the drive is mounted then the loop is entered. The existence of the file is checked every minute to see if it is time to begin the backup.

- When the file is found the `backup1` script (see next) is run. The output from it is sent to both the screen and the file using the `tee` command.

- The date format specifier `'+%Y%m%d'` shows the date in this format: YYYYMMDD

I check the files in the `/data/mainlogs` directory from time to time to make sure my backups are being created correctly with no errors.

The following script is used to backup my system. The logic here is the current day backups are stored on the hard drive in the `$TDIR` directory. They are also copied to a numbered directory on the external drive. These go into directories numbered 1 through 7. When the last one is reached it starts back at 1 again. This way there are always 7 days of backups available on the external drive.

This script must also be run as root:

Chapter 6 - Script 7

```
#!/bin/sh
#    Jim's backup program
#    Runs standalone
#    Copies to /data/backups first, then to USB backup drive
VER="File backup by Jim Lewis 5/27/2017 A"
TDIR=/data/backups
RUNDIR=$LDIR/backup
DR=/wd1
echo $VER
cd $RUNDIR
# Insure backup drive is mounted
file $DR | grep broken
a=$?
if [ "$a" != "1" ] ; then
  echo "ERROR: USB drive $DR is not mounted!!!!!!!!!!!!!!!"
  beep
  exit 255
fi
date >> datelog.txt
date
echo "Removing files from $TDIR"
```

```
cd "$TDIR"
rc=$?
if [ $rc -ne 0 ] ; then
 echo "backup1: Error cannot change to $TDIR!"
 exit 250
fi
rm *.gz
echo "Backing up files to $TDIR"
X=`date '+%Y%m%d'`
cd /
tar cvzf "$TDIR/lewis$X.gz"  lewis
tar cvzf "$TDIR/temp$X.gz"   temp
tar cvzf "$TDIR/root$X.gz"   root
cd /home
tar cvzf "$TDIR/guest$X.gz" --exclude=Cache --exclude=.cache --exclude=.
evolution --exclude=vmware --exclude=.thumbnails  --exclude=.gconf
--exclude=.kde --exclude=.adobe  --exclude=.mozilla  --exclude=.
gconf  --exclude=thunderbird  --exclude=.local --exclude=.macromedia
--exclude=.config   guest1
cd $RUNDIR
T=`cat filenum1`
BACKDIR=$DR/backups/$T
rm $BACKDIR/*.gz
cd "$TDIR"
cp *.gz $BACKDIR
echo $VER
cd $BACKDIR
pwd
ls -lah
cd $RUNDIR
let T++
if [ $T -gt 7 ] ; then
 T=1
fi
echo $T > filenum1
```

This is a bit more complicated than the previous scripts so let's go through it line by line:

- The RUNDIR variable holds the starting directory for the scripts.
- The DR variable points to the external backup drive.
- The drive is checked to insure it is mounted.
- The current date is appended to the datelog.txt file.
- The TDIR variable is the target directory for the backups.
- A cd is performed to that directory and the return code is checked. On error the script exits with a 250.
- The backups from the previous day are deleted.

It now goes back to the / directory to perform the tar backups.

Notice that several directories are excluded from the guest1 directory.

- The cd $RUNDIR puts it back into the starting directory.
- The T=`filenum1` gets the value from that file and puts it into the T variable. This is a counter for which directory to use next on the external drive.
- BACKDIR is set to the old backups and then they are removed.
- Control returns again to the starting directory, and the current backups are copied to the appropriate directory on the external drive.
- The version of the program is displayed again so that it can be easily found on a cluttered screen.
- Control goes to the backup directory, the pwd displays the name, and then the contents of the directory are displayed.
- The T variable is incremented by 1. If it is greater than 7 it is set back to 1.

And finally the updated T variable is written back to the filenum1 file.

This script should serve as a good starting point for whatever backup process you want to develop. Note that the scp command can be used to copy files directly to another computer without user intervention. This will be covered in *Chapter 10, Scripting Best Practices*.

Summary

We described how to create a script to automate a task. The proper way to use cron to run a script automatically at a specific time was covered. The archive commands zip and tar were discussed to show how to perform compressed backups. A full scheduler and backup script were also included and discussed.

In the next chapter we will show how to read and write files in a script.

7
Working with Files

This chapter will show how to read from and write to text files. It will also cover file encryption and checksums.

The topics covered in this chapter are as follows:

- Show how to write out a file using the redirection operator
- Show how to read a file
- Explain how the output from a command can be captured and used in a script
- Go over `cat` and other important commands
- Cover file encryption and checksum programs such as sum and OpenSSL

Writing files

We showed in some of the previous chapters how to create and write files by using the redirection operator. To recap, this command will create the file `ifconfig.txt` (or overwrite the file if it already exists):

```
ifconfig  >  ifconfig.txt
```

The following command will append to any previous file or create a new one if it does not already exist:

```
ifconfig  >>  ifconfig.txt
```

Some of the previous scripts used the back-tick operator to retrieve the data from a file. Let's recap by looking at *Script 1*:

Chapter 7 - Script 1

```
#!/bin/sh
#
# 6/1/2017
#
echo "Chapter 7 - Script 1"
FN=file1.txt
rm $FN 2> /dev/null          # remove it silently if it exists
x=1
while [ $x -le 10 ]          # 10 lines
do
 echo "x: $x"
 echo "Line $x" >> $FN       # append to file
 let x++
done
echo "End of script1"
exit 0
```

Here is a screenshot:

```
guest1@big1:~/LinuxScriptingBook/chapters/chap7
File  Edit  View  Search  Terminal  Help
guest1 ~/LinuxScriptingBook/chapters/chap7 $ script1
Chapter 7 - Script 1
x: 1
x: 2
x: 3
x: 4
x: 5
x: 6
x: 7
x: 8
x: 9
x: 10
End of script1
guest1 ~/LinuxScriptingBook/chapters/chap7 $ cat file1.txt
Line 1
Line 2
Line 3
Line 4
Line 5
Line 6
Line 7
Line 8
Line 9
Line 10
guest1 ~/LinuxScriptingBook/chapters/chap7 $
```

This is pretty straight forward. It removes the file (silently) if it exists, and then outputs each line to the file, incrementing x each time. When x gets to 10 the loop terminates.

Reading files

Now let's look again at the method the backup scripts in the last chapter used to get the value from a file:

Chapter 7 - Script 2

```
#!/bin/sh
#
# 6/2/2017
#
echo "Chapter 7 - Script 2"

FN=filenum1.txt            # input/output filename
MAXFILES=5                 # maximum number before going back to 1

if [ ! -f $FN ] ; then
   echo 1 > $FN            # create the file if it does not exist
fi

echo -n "Contents of $FN: "
cat $FN                    # display the contents

count=`cat $FN`            # put the output of cat into variable count
echo "Initial value of count from $FN: $count"

let count++
if [ $count -gt $MAXFILES ] ; then
  count=1
fi

echo "New value of count: $count"
```

```
echo $count > $FN


echo -n "New contents of $FN: "
cat $FN


echo "End of script2"
exit 0
```

Here is the screenshot for *Script 2*:

```
 guest1@big1:~/LinuxScriptingBook/chapters/chap7
 File  Edit  View  Search  Terminal  Help
guest1 ~/LinuxScriptingBook/chapters/chap7 $ rm filenum1.txt
guest1 ~/LinuxScriptingBook/chapters/chap7 $ script2
Chapter 7 - Script 2
Contents of filenum1.txt: 1
Initial value of count from filenum1.txt: 1
New value of count: 2
New contents of filenum1.txt: 2
End of script2
guest1 ~/LinuxScriptingBook/chapters/chap7 $ script2
Chapter 7 - Script 2
Contents of filenum1.txt: 2
Initial value of count from filenum1.txt: 2
New value of count: 3
New contents of filenum1.txt: 3
End of script2
guest1 ~/LinuxScriptingBook/chapters/chap7 $ script2
Chapter 7 - Script 2
Contents of filenum1.txt: 3
Initial value of count from filenum1.txt: 3
New value of count: 4
New contents of filenum1.txt: 4
End of script2
guest1 ~/LinuxScriptingBook/chapters/chap7 $ script2
Chapter 7 - Script 2
Contents of filenum1.txt: 4
Initial value of count from filenum1.txt: 4
New value of count: 5
New contents of filenum1.txt: 5
End of script2
guest1 ~/LinuxScriptingBook/chapters/chap7 $ script2
Chapter 7 - Script 2
Contents of filenum1.txt: 5
Initial value of count from filenum1.txt: 5
New value of count: 1
New contents of filenum1.txt: 1
End of script2
guest1 ~/LinuxScriptingBook/chapters/chap7 $ 
```

We start by setting the `FN` variable to the name of the file (`filenum1.txt`). It is displayed by the `cat` command and then the contents of the file are assigned to the `count` variable. It is displayed and then incremented by 1. The new value is written back to the file and then it is displayed again. Run this one at least 6 times to see how it wraps around.

This is just one simple way to create and read a file. Now let's look at a script that reads several lines from a file. It will use the file `file1.txt` that was created by the preceding *Script 1*.

Chapter 7 - Script 3

```sh
#!/bin/sh
#
# 6/1/2017
#
echo "Chapter 7 - Script 3"
FN=file1.txt                  # filename
while IFS= read -r linevar    # use read to put line into linevar
do
   echo "$linevar"            # display contents of linevar
done < $FN                    # the file to use as input
echo "End of script3"
exit 0
```

And here is the output:

```
guest1@big1:~/LinuxScriptingBook/chapters/chap7
 File  Edit  View  Search  Terminal  Help
guest1 ~/LinuxScriptingBook/chapters/chap7 $ script3
Chapter 7 - Script 3
Line 1
Line 2
Line 3
Line 4
Line 5
Line 6
Line 7
Line 8
Line 9
Line 10
End of script3
guest1 ~/LinuxScriptingBook/chapters/chap7 $
```

The structure here may look a little strange as it is rather different from what we have seen before. This script uses the `read` command to get each line of the file. In the statement:

```
while IFS= read -r linevar
```

The `IFS=` (**Internal Field Separator**) prevents `read` from trimming leading and trailing whitespace characters. The `-r` parameter to read causes backslash escape sequences to be ignored. The next line uses the redirection operator to enable `file1.txt` as the input for `read`.

```
done   <   $FN
```

There is a lot of new material here and so look this over carefully until you get comfortable with it.

There is a slight flaw in the above script. If the file does not exist an error will occur. Look at the following screenshot:

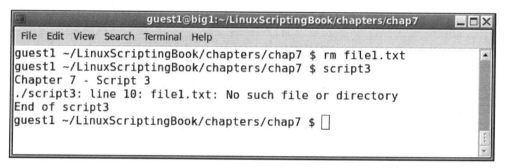

Shell scripts are interpreted, meaning each line is examined and run by the system one at a time. This is different from say a program written in the C language which is compiled. This means any syntax errors will appear during the compile stage and not when the program is run. We will discuss how to avoid most shell scripting syntax errors in *Chapter 9, Debugging scripts*.

Here is *Script 4* with a solution to the missing file problem:

Chapter 7 - Script 4

```
#!/bin/sh
#
# 6/1/2017
#
```

```
echo "Chapter 7 - Script 4"


FN=file1.txt                    # filename
if [ ! -f $FN ] ; then
 echo "File $FN does not exist."
 exit 100
fi


while IFS= read -r linevar    # use read to put line into linevar
do
   echo "$linevar"            # display contents of linevar
done < $FN                    # the file to use as input


echo "End of script4"
exit 0
```

And the following is the output:

```
guest1@big1:~/LinuxScriptingBook/chapters/chap7
File  Edit  View  Search  Terminal  Help
guest1 ~/LinuxScriptingBook/chapters/chap7 $ script4
Chapter 7 - Script 4
File file1.txt does not exist.
guest1 ~/LinuxScriptingBook/chapters/chap7 $ script1
Chapter 7 - Script 1
x: 1
x: 2
x: 3
x: 4
x: 5
x: 6
x: 7
x: 8
x: 9
x: 10
End of script1
guest1 ~/LinuxScriptingBook/chapters/chap7 $ script4
Chapter 7 - Script 4
Line 1
Line 2
Line 3
Line 4
Line 5
Line 6
Line 7
Line 8
Line 9
Line 10
End of script4
guest1 ~/LinuxScriptingBook/chapters/chap7 $
```

Keep this in mind when using files and always check to make sure the file exists before trying to read it.

Reading and writing files

This next script reads a text file and creates a copy of it:

Chapter 7 - Script 5

```
#!/bin/sh
#
# 6/1/2017
#
echo "Chapter 7 - Script 5"

if [ $# -ne 2 ] ; then
  echo "Usage: script5 infile outfile"
  echo " Copies text file infile to outfile."
  exit 255
fi


INFILE=$1
OUTFILE=$2


if [ ! -f $INFILE ] ; then
  echo "Error: File $INFILE does not exist."
  exit 100
fi


if [ $INFILE = $OUTFILE ] ; then
  echo "Error: Cannot copy to same file."
  exit 101
fi


rm $OUTFILE 2> /dev/null        # remove it
```

```
echo "Reading file $INFILE ..."

x=0
while IFS= read -r linevar      # use read to put line into linevar
do
  echo "$linevar" >> $OUTFILE   # append to file
  let x++
done < $INFILE                  # the file to use as input
echo "$x lines read."

diff $INFILE $OUTFILE           # use diff to check the output
rc=$?
if [ $rc -ne 0 ] ; then
 echo "Error, files do not match."
 exit 103
else
 echo "File $OUTFILE created."
fi

sum $INFILE $OUTFILE            # show the checksums

echo "End of script5"
exit $rc
```

Here is the screenshot for *Script 5*:

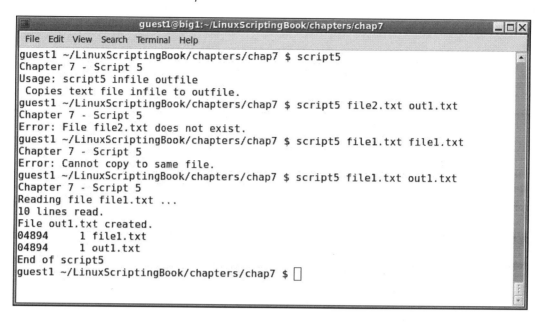

```
guest1@big1:~/LinuxScriptingBook/chapters/chap7
File  Edit  View  Search  Terminal  Help
guest1 ~/LinuxScriptingBook/chapters/chap7 $ script5
Chapter 7 - Script 5
Usage: script5 infile outfile
 Copies text file infile to outfile.
guest1 ~/LinuxScriptingBook/chapters/chap7 $ script5 file2.txt out1.txt
Chapter 7 - Script 5
Error: File file2.txt does not exist.
guest1 ~/LinuxScriptingBook/chapters/chap7 $ script5 file1.txt file1.txt
Chapter 7 - Script 5
Error: Cannot copy to same file.
guest1 ~/LinuxScriptingBook/chapters/chap7 $ script5 file1.txt out1.txt
Chapter 7 - Script 5
Reading file file1.txt ...
10 lines read.
File out1.txt created.
04894     1 file1.txt
04894     1 out1.txt
End of script5
guest1 ~/LinuxScriptingBook/chapters/chap7 $ []
```

This shows how to read and write a text file in a script. The following explains each line:

- The script starts by checking if two parameters were given and if not the Usage message is displayed.

- It then checks if the input file exists and exits with code 100 if it does not.

- A check is made to insure the user is not trying to copy to the same file, because a syntax error at line 34 would have occurred. This code insures that will not happen.

- The output file is removed if it exists. This is because we want to copy to a new file and not append to an existing one.

- The while loop reads and writes the lines. A count is made of the number of lines in x.

- When the loops ends the number of lines is output.

- As a sanity check, the diff command is used to make sure the files are the same.

- And as an added check the sum command is run on the two files.

Reading and writing files interactively

This next script is similar to one in Chapter 5, Creating Interactive Scripts. It reads the file specified, displays a form, and allows the user to edit and then save it:

Chapter 7 - Script 6

```sh
#!/bin/sh
# 6/2/2017
# Chapter 7 - Script 6

trap catchCtrlC INT          # Initialize the trap

# Subroutines
catchCtrlC()
{
  move 13 0
  savefile
  movestr 23 0 "Script terminated by user."
  echo ""                    # carriage return
  exit 0
}

cls()
{
  tput clear
}

move()                       # move cursor to row, col
{
  tput cup $1 $2
}

movestr()                    # move cursor to row, col
{
  tput cup $1 $2
```

```
    echo -n "$3"                # display string
}


checktermsize()
{
 rc1=0                         # default is no error
 if [[ $LINES -lt $1 || $COLUMNS -lt $2 ]] ; then
  rc1=1                        # set return code
 fi
 return $rc1
}


init()                         # set up the cursor position array
{
 srow[0]=2;  scol[0]=7         # name
 srow[1]=4;  scol[1]=12        # address 1
 srow[2]=6;  scol[2]=12        # address 2
 srow[3]=8;  scol[3]=7         # city
 srow[4]=8;  scol[4]=37        # state
 srow[5]=8;  scol[5]=52        # zip code
 srow[6]=10; scol[6]=8         # email
}


drawscreen()                   # main screen draw routine
{
 cls                           # clear the screen
 movestr 0 25 "Chapter 7 - Script 6"

 movestr 2 1  "Name: ${array[0]}"
 movestr 4 1  "Address 1: ${array[1]}"
 movestr 6 1  "Address 2: ${array[2]}"
 movestr 8 1  "City: ${array[3]}"
 movestr 8 30 "State: ${array[4]}"
 movestr 8 42 "Zip code: ${array[5]}"
```

```
 movestr 10 1 "Email: ${array[6]}"
}


getdata()
{
 x=0                                 # start at the first field
 while [ true ]
 do
  row=${srow[x]}; col=${scol[x]}
  move $row $col
  read var
  if [ -n "$var" ] ; then      # if not blank assign to array
    array[$x]=$var
  fi
  let x++
  if [ $x -eq $sizeofarray ] ; then
   x=0                               # go back to first field
  fi
 done


 return 0
}


savefile()
{
 rm $FN 2> /dev/null          # remove any existing file
 echo "Writing file $FN ..."
 y=0
 while [ $y -lt $sizeofarray ]
 do
  echo "$y - '${array[$y]}'"                # display to screen
  echo "${array[$y]}" >> "$FN"              # write to file
  let y++
 done
 echo "File written."
 return 0
```

```
}

getfile()
{
 x=0
 if [ -n "$FN" ] ; then        # check that file exists
  while IFS= read -r linevar  # use read to put line into linevar
  do
   array[$x]="$linevar"
   let x++
  done < $FN                  # the file to use as input
 fi
 return 0
}


# Code starts here
if [ $# -ne 1 ] ; then
 echo "Usage: script6 file"
 echo " Reads existing file or creates a new file"
 echo " and allows user to enter data into fields."
 echo " Press Ctrl-C to end."
 exit 255
fi


FN=$1                        # filename (input and output)
sizeofarray=7                # number of array elements
checktermsize 25 80
rc=$?
if [ $rc -ne 0 ] ; then
 echo "Please size the terminal to 25x80 and try again."
 exit 1
fi


init                         # initialize the screen array
getfile                      # read in file if it exists
```

```
drawscreen                      # draw the screen
getdata                         # read in the data and put into the fields


exit 0
```

Here is what this looks like on my system:

Here is a description of the code:

- The first thing that gets set up in this script is a trap of *Ctrl + C* which causes the file to be saved and the script to end.

- The subroutines are defined.

- The `getdata` routine is used to read the user input.

- The `savefile` routine writes out the data array.

- The `getfile` routine reads the file, if it exists, into the array.

- The parameters are checked as one filename is required.

- The FN variable is set to the name of the file.

- When using arrays it's a good idea to have a set size, that is, `sizeofarray`.

- The size of the terminal is checked to make sure it is 25x80 (or 80x25 depending on your GUI).
- The `init` routine is called which sets up the screen array.
- The routines `getfile` and `drawscreen` are called.
- The `getdata` routine is used to move the cursor and get the data from the fields into the proper array location.
- *Ctrl* + *C* is used to save the file and terminate the script.

This is an example of how a simple screen input/output routine can be developed in Bash. This script could use a few refinements, here is a partial list:

- Check an existing file for a specific header. This could help insure the file is in the correct format and avoid a syntax error.
- Check the input file to make sure it is text and not binary. Hint: Use the file and `grep` commands.
- If the file cannot be written out properly make sure to catch the error gracefully.

File checksums

You probably noticed the use of the `sum` command above. It displays the checksum and block count of files which can be used to determine if two or more files are the same file (that is, have the exact same contents).

Here is a real world example:

Suppose you are writing a book, and the files are being sent from the author to the publisher for review. The publisher makes some revisions and then sends the revised file back to the author. It is sometimes easy to get out of sync, and receive a file that doesn't look any different. If you run the `sum` command against the two files you can easily determine if they are the same.

Take a look at the following screenshot:

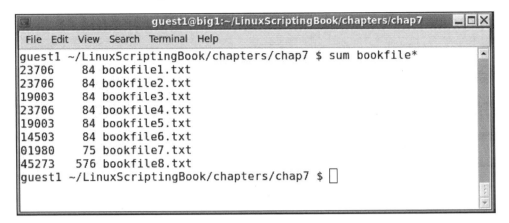

```
guest1@big1:~/LinuxScriptingBook/chapters/chap7          _ □ X

File  Edit  View  Search  Terminal  Help
guest1 ~/LinuxScriptingBook/chapters/chap7 $ sum bookfile*
23706     84 bookfile1.txt
23706     84 bookfile2.txt
19003     84 bookfile3.txt
23706     84 bookfile4.txt
19003     84 bookfile5.txt
14503     84 bookfile6.txt
01980     75 bookfile7.txt
45273    576 bookfile8.txt
guest1 ~/LinuxScriptingBook/chapters/chap7 $ []
```

The first column is the checksum and the second column is the block count. If both of these are the same that means the contents of the files are identical. So, in this example bookfiles 1, 2, and 4 are the same. Bookfiles 3 and 5 are also the same. However, bookfiles 6, 7, and 8 don't match up with anything, and the last two don't even have the same block count.

> Note: The sum command only looks at the contents and block count of the files. It does not look at the filename or other file attributes such as ownership or permissions. To do that you could use the ls and stat commands.

File encryption

There are times you might want to encrypt some important and/or confidential files on your system. Some people store their passwords in a file on their computers, this is probably okay but only if some type of file encryption is being used. There are many encryption programs available, here we will show OpenSSL.

The OpenSSL command line tool is very popular and is most likely already installed on your computer (it came by default on my CentOS 6.8 systems). It has several options and methods of encryption, however we will cover just the basics.

Using `file1.txt` again from above try the following on your system:

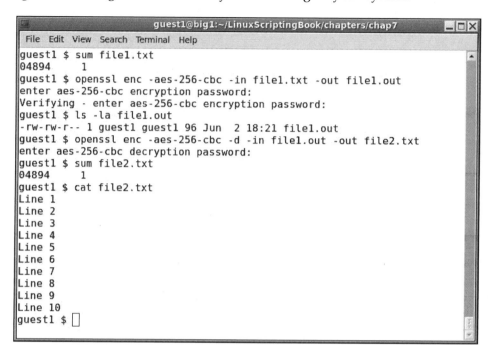

```
guest1@big1:~/LinuxScriptingBook/chapters/chap7
File  Edit  View  Search  Terminal  Help
guest1 $ sum file1.txt
04894     1
guest1 $ openssl enc -aes-256-cbc -in file1.txt -out file1.out
enter aes-256-cbc encryption password:
Verifying - enter aes-256-cbc encryption password:
guest1 $ ls -la file1.out
-rw-rw-r-- 1 guest1 guest1 96 Jun  2 18:21 file1.out
guest1 $ openssl enc -aes-256-cbc -d -in file1.out -out file2.txt
enter aes-256-cbc decryption password:
guest1 $ sum file2.txt
04894     1
guest1 $ cat file2.txt
Line 1
Line 2
Line 3
Line 4
Line 5
Line 6
Line 7
Line 8
Line 9
Line 10
guest1 $
```

We start by performing a sum on the `file1.txt` file, then run `openssl`. Here is the syntax:

- `enc`: specify which encoding to use, in this case it's `aes-256-cbc`
- `-in:` the input file
- `-out`: the output file
- `-d`: decrypt

After running the `openssl` command we perform an `ls -la` to verify that the output file was indeed created.

We then decrypt the file. Note the order of the files and the addition of the `-d` parameter (to decrypt). We do another sum to verify that the resulting file is the same as the original.

Since there is no way I am going to type that all the time let's write a quick script to do it:

Chapter 7 - Script 7

```sh
#!/bin/sh
#
# 6/2/2017
#
echo "Chapter 7 - Script 7"

if [ $# -ne 3 ] ; then
  echo "Usage: script7 -e|-d infile outfile"
  echo " Uses openssl to encrypt files."
  echo " -e to encrypt"
  echo " -d to decrypt"
  exit 255
fi


PARM=$1
INFILE=$2
OUTFILE=$3

if [ ! -f $INFILE ] ; then
  echo "Input file $INFILE does not exist."
  exit 100
fi


if [ "$PARM" = "-e" ] ; then
  echo "Encrypting"
  openssl enc -aes-256-cbc -in $INFILE -out $OUTFILE
elif [ "$PARM" = "-d" ] ; then
  echo "Decrypting"
  openssl enc -aes-256-cbc -d -in $INFILE -out $OUTFILE
else
```

```
echo "Please specify either -e or -d."
exit 101
fi


ls -la $OUTFILE


echo "End of script7"
exit 0
```

Here is the screenshot:

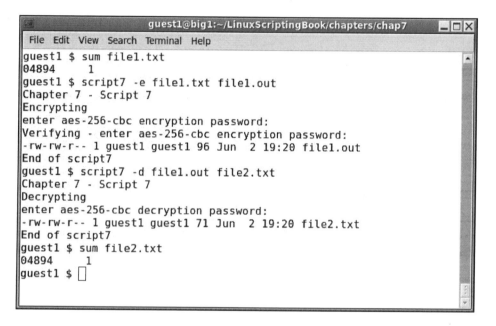

This is obviously a lot easier than typing (or trying to remember) the syntax for openssl. As you can see the resulting decrypted file (file2.txt) is the same as the file1.txt file.

Summary

In this chapter we showed how to write out a file using the redirection operator and how to read a file using the (properly formatted) read command. Converting the contents of a file into a variable was covered as was the use of checksums and file encryption.

In the next chapter we will look at some utilities that can be used to gather information from web pages on the Internet.

8

Working with wget and curl

This chapter will show how to use `wget` and `curl` to gather information directly from the internet.

The topics covered in this chapter are:

- Show how to get information using `wget`.
- Show how to get information using `curl`.

Scripts that can gather data in this way can be very powerful tools to have at your disposal. As you will see from this chapter, you can get stock quotes, lake levels, just about anything automatically from web sites anywhere in the world.

Introducing the wget program

You may have already heard about or even used the `wget` program. It is a command line utility that can be used to download files from the Internet.

Here is a screenshot showing `wget` in its most simplest form:

```
                  guest1@big1:~/LinuxScriptingBook/chapters/chap8        _ □ X
 File  Edit  View  Search  Terminal  Help
 guest1 ~/LinuxScriptingBook/chapters/chap8 $ wget http://jklewis.com
 --2017-06-03 16:43:46--  http://jklewis.com/
 Resolving jklewis.com... 66.96.149.17
 Connecting to jklewis.com|66.96.149.17|:80... connected.
 HTTP request sent, awaiting response... 200 OK
 Length: 1560 (1.5K) [text/html]
 Saving to: "index.html"

 100%[================================>] 1,560       --.-K/s    in 0s

 2017-06-03 16:43:46 (188 MB/s) - "index.html" saved [1560/1560]

 guest1 ~/LinuxScriptingBook/chapters/chap8 $ █
```

wget options

In the output you can see that wget downloaded the index.html file from my jklewis.com website.

This is the default behavior of wget. The standard usage is:

```
wget [options] URL
```

where **URL** stands for **Uniform Resource Locator,** or address of the website.

Here is just a short list of the many available options with wget:

Parameter	Explanation
-o	log file, messages will be written here instead of to STDOUT
-a	same as -o excepts it appends to the log file
-O	output file, copy the file to this name
-d	turn debugging on
-q	quiet mode
-v	verbose mode
-r	recursive mode

Let's try another example:

```
guest1@big1:~/LinuxScriptingBook/chapters/chap8
File  Edit  View  Search  Terminal  Help
guest1 ~/LinuxScriptingBook/chapters/chap8 $ wget -o log1.txt http://jklewis.com
guest1 ~/LinuxScriptingBook/chapters/chap8 $ echo $?
0
guest1 ~/LinuxScriptingBook/chapters/chap8 $ cat log1.txt
--2017-06-05 12:37:10--  http://jklewis.com/
Resolving jklewis.com... 66.96.149.17
Connecting to jklewis.com|66.96.149.17|:80... connected.
HTTP request sent, awaiting response... 200 OK
Length: 1560 (1.5K) [text/html]
Saving to: "index.html.1"

    0K .                                               100%  191M=0s

2017-06-05 12:37:10 (191 MB/s) - "index.html.1" saved [1560/1560]

guest1 ~/LinuxScriptingBook/chapters/chap8 $
```

The -o option was used in this case. The return code was checked and a code of 0 means no failure. There was no output because it was directed to the log file which was displayed by the cat command.

The -o option, write output to file, was used in this case. There was no output displayed because it was directed to the log file which was then shown by the cat command. The return code from wget was checked and a code of 0 means no failure.

Notice that this time it named the downloaded file index.html.1. This is because index.html was created in the previous example. The author of this application did it this way to avoid overwriting a previously downloaded file. Very nice!

Take a look at this next example:

```
guest1@big1:~/LinuxScriptingBook/chapters/chap8
File  Edit  View  Search  Terminal  Help
guest1 ~/LinuxScriptingBook/chapters/chap8 $ wget http://jklewis.com/shipfire.gif
--2017-06-05 14:33:31--  http://jklewis.com/shipfire.gif
Resolving jklewis.com... 66.96.149.17
Connecting to jklewis.com|66.96.149.17|:80... connected.
HTTP request sent, awaiting response... 200 OK
Length: 994 [image/gif]
Saving to: "shipfire.gif"

100%[====================================>] 994         --.-K/s    in 0s

2017-06-05 14:33:31 (38.8 MB/s) - "shipfire.gif" saved [994/994]

guest1 ~/LinuxScriptingBook/chapters/chap8 $ ls -la shipfire.gif
-rw-rw-r-- 1 guest1 guest1 994 Jan 29  2004 shipfire.gif
guest1 ~/LinuxScriptingBook/chapters/chap8 $ ☐
```

Here we are telling wget to download the file given (shipfire.gif).

In this next screenshot we show how wget will return a useful error code:

```
guest1@big1:~/LinuxScriptingBook/chapters/chap8
File  Edit  View  Search  Terminal  Help
guest1 ~/LinuxScriptingBook/chapters/chap8 $ wget http://jklewis.com/shipfire100.gif
--2017-06-05 14:36:58--  http://jklewis.com/shipfire100.gif
Resolving jklewis.com... 66.96.149.17
Connecting to jklewis.com|66.96.149.17|:80... connected.
HTTP request sent, awaiting response... 404 Not Found
2017-06-05 14:36:58 ERROR 404: Not Found.

guest1 ~/LinuxScriptingBook/chapters/chap8 $ echo $?
8
guest1 ~/LinuxScriptingBook/chapters/chap8 $ stat shipfire100.gif
stat: cannot stat `shipfire100.gif': No such file or directory
guest1 ~/LinuxScriptingBook/chapters/chap8 $ ☐
```

wget return codes

This error occurred because there is no file named `shipfire100.gif` in the base directory on my website. Notice how the output shows a **404 Not Found** message, this is seen very often on the Web. In general, it means a requested resource was not available at that time. In this case the file isn't there and so that message appears.

Note too how `wget` returned an `8` error code. The man page for `wget` shows this for the possible exit codes from `wget`:

Error codes	Explanation
0	No problems occurred.
1	Generic error code.
2	Parse error. For instance when parsing command-line options, the `.wgetrc` or `.netrc` files
3	File I/O error.
4	Network failure.
5	SSL verification failure.
6	Username/password authentication failure.
7	Protocol errors.
8	Server issued an error response.

A return of `8` makes pretty good sense. The server could not find the file and so returned a `404` error code.

wget configuration files

Now is a good time to mention the different `wget` configuration files. There are two main files, `/etc/wgetrc` is the default location of the global `wget` startup file. In most cases you probably should not edit this unless you really want to make changes that affect all users. The file `$HOME/.wgetrc` is a better place to put any options you would like. A good way to do this is to open both `/etc/wgetrc` and `$HOME/.wgetrc` in your text editor and then copy the stanzas you want into your `$HOME./wgetrc` file.

For more information on the `wget` config files consult the `man` page (`man wget`).

Now let's see `wget` in action. I wrote this a while back to keep track of the water level in the lake I used to go boating in:

Chapter 8 - Script 1

```
#!/bin/sh
# 6/5/2017
# Chapter 8 - Script 1

URL=http://www.arlut.utexas.edu/omg/weather.html
FN=weather.html
TF=temp1.txt                # temp file
LF=logfile.txt              # log file

loop=1
while [ $loop -eq 1 ]
do
 rm $FN 2> /dev/null         # remove old file
 wget -o $LF $URL
 rc=$?
 if [ $rc -ne 0 ] ; then
   echo "wget returned code: $rc"
   echo "logfile:"
   cat $LF

   exit 200
 fi

 date
 grep "Lake Travis Level:" $FN > $TF
 cat $TF | cut  -d ' ' -f 12 --complement

 sleep 1h
done

exit 0
```

This output is from June 5, 2017. It's not much to look at but here it is:

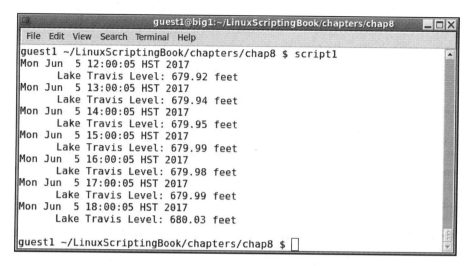

You can see from the script and the output that it runs once every hour. In case you were wondering why anyone would write something like this, I needed to know if the lake level went below 640 feet as I would have had to move my boat out of the marina. This was during a severe drought back in Texas.

There are a few things to keep in mind when writing a script like this:

- When first writing the script perform the wget once manually and then work with the downloaded file.

- Do not use wget several times in a short period of time or else you may get blocked by the site.

- Keep in mind that HTML programmers like to change things all the time and so you may have to adjust your script accordingly.

- When you finally get the script just right be sure to activate the wget again.

wget and recursion

The wget program can also be used to download the contents of an entire website by using the recursive (-r) option.

For an example look at the following screenshot:

```
root@big1:/home/guest1/LinuxScriptingBook/chapters/chap8          _ □ X
File  Edit  View  Search  Terminal  Help
big1 /data # wget -r -nv -o log1.txt http://lewisjk.com
big1 /data # more log1.txt
2017-06-05 19:02:26 URL:http://lewisjk.com/ [1560/1560] -> "lewisjk.com/index.html" [
1]
2017-06-05 19:02:27 URL:http://lewisjk.com/shipfire.gif [994/994] -> "lewisjk.com/shi
pfire.gif" [1]
2017-06-05 19:02:27 URL:http://lewisjk.com/Lewis_Resume20170323.html [18572/18572] ->
 "lewisjk.com/Lewis_Resume20170323.html" [1]
2017-06-05 19:02:27 URL:http://lewisjk.com/Lewis_Resume20170323.doc [34304/34304] ->
"lewisjk.com/Lewis_Resume20170323.doc" [1]
2017-06-05 19:02:27 URL:http://lewisjk.com/spacegame/index.html [767/767] -> "lewisjk
.com/spacegame/index.html" [1]
2017-06-05 19:02:28 URL:http://lewisjk.com/subgame/index.html [2575/2575] -> "lewisjk
.com/subgame/index.html" [1]
2017-06-05 19:02:28 URL:http://lewisjk.com/lunar/betas/ [1903/1903] -> "lewisjk.com/l
unar/betas" [1]
2017-06-05 19:02:28 URL:http://lewisjk.com/targ/ [1836/1836] -> "lewisjk.com/targ" [1
]
2017-06-05 19:02:28 URL:http://lewisjk.com/tegoa/ [3028/3028] -> "lewisjk.com/tegoa"
[1]
2017-06-05 19:02:28 URL:http://lewisjk.com/os2/ [6593/6593] -> "lewisjk.com/os2" [1]
2017-06-05 19:02:29 URL:http://lewisjk.com/spacegame/opening-screen.png [96797/96797]
 -> "lewisjk.com/spacegame/opening-screen.png" [1]
2017-06-05 19:02:30 URL:http://lewisjk.com/spacegame/Screenshot-32.png [1036760/10367
60] -> "lewisjk.com/spacegame/Screenshot-32.png" [1]
2017-06-05 19:02:30 URL:http://lewisjk.com/spacegame/Screenshot-33.png [979374/979374
] -> "lewisjk.com/spacegame/Screenshot-33.png" [1]
2017-06-05 19:02:30 URL:http://lewisjk.com/spacegame/Screenshot-38.png [880885/880885
] -> "lewisjk.com/spacegame/Screenshot-38.png" [1]
2017-06-05 19:02:30 URL:http://lewisjk.com/spacegame/Screenshot-40.png [897204/897204
] -> "lewisjk.com/spacegame/Screenshot-40.png" [1]
2017-06-05 19:02:30 URL:http://lewisjk.com/spacegame/spacegame.html [260/260] -> "lew
isjk.com/spacegame/spacegame.html" [1]
2017-06-05 19:02:30 URL:http://lewisjk.com/subgame/tegoa.css [100/100] -> "lewisjk.co
m/subgame/tegoa.css" [1]
2017-06-05 19:02:30 URL:http://lewisjk.com/subgame/beta4/subgame.html [255/255] -> "l
ewisjk.com/subgame/beta4/subgame.html" [1]
2017-06-05 19:02:31 URL:http://lewisjk.com/subgame/Screenshot-10.png [570668/570668]
--More--(32%)
```

The no verbose (-nv) option was used to limit the output. After the wget command completed the more command was used to view the contents of the log. Depending on the number of files the output might be very long.

When using wget you may run into unexpected issues. It may not get any files, or it may get some but not all of them. It might even fail without any reasonable error message. If this happens check the man page (man wget) very carefully. There may be an option that can help get you through the problem. In particular look at the following.

Run wget --version on your system. It will display a detailed listing of the options and features and also how wget was compiled.

Here is an example taken from my system running CentOS 6.8 64-bit:

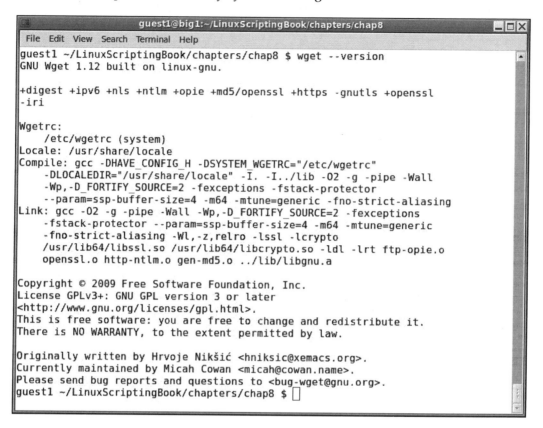

wget options

Normally the defaults used by wget are good enough for most users, however, you may need to tweak things from time to time to get it to work the way you want it to.

Here is a partial list of some of the wget options:

wget option	Explanation
-o filename	Output messages to a log file. This was covered earlier in the chapter.
-t number	Try number times before giving up on the connection.
-c	Continue to download a partially downloaded file from a previous wget.
-S	Display the headers sent by the server.

wget option	Explanation
-Q number	The quota, or total amount of bytes that will be downloaded. Number can be in bytes, kilobytes (k), or megabytes (m). Set to 0 or inf for no quota.
-l number	This specifies the maximum recursion level. The default is 5.
-m	This is good for when trying to create a mirror of a site. It is equivalent to using the -r -N -l inf --no-remove-listing options.

Another thing you may try is to turn on debugging with the -d option. Note that this will only work if your version of wget was compiled with debug support. Let's see what happens when I try it on my system:

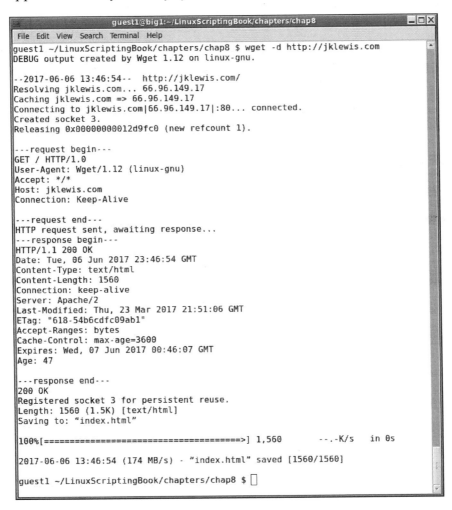

I wasn't sure if debugging was turned on or not, now I know. This output might not be very useful unless you are a developer, however, if you ever need to send in a bug report on wget they are going to ask for the debug output.

As you can see, wget is a very powerful program with several options.

> Remember to use wget with care and do not forget to put a sleep of at least a minute in your loop. An hour would be even better.

curl

Now let's look at the curl program as it is somewhat similar to wget. One of the main differences between wget and curl is how they handle the output.

The wget program by default displays some progress information on the screen and then downloads the index.html file. In contrast, curl normally displays the file itself on the screen.

Here is an example of curl running on my system using my favorite website (screenshot shortened to save space):

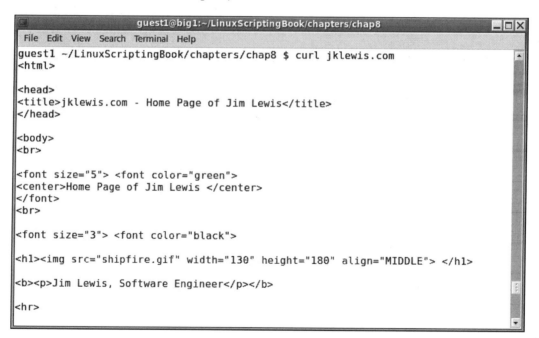

Another way to get the output into a file is by using redirection like this:

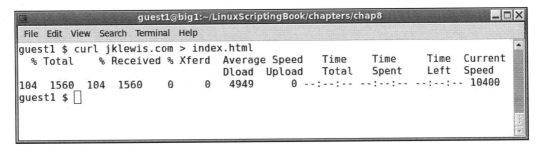

You will notice that when redirected to a file the transfer progress is displayed on the screen. Also note that any error output goes into the file if redirected and not the screen.

curl options

Here is a very brief list of the options available in curl:

Curl options	Explanation
-o	Output filename
-s	Silent mode. Shows nothing, not even errors
-S	Show errors if in silent mode
-v	Verbose, useful for debugging

There are many other options to `curl`, as well as several pages of return codes. For more information consult the `curl man` page.

And now here is a script showing how curl can be used to automatically get the current value of the Dow Jones Industrial Average:

Chapter 8 - Script 2

```
#!/bin/sh
# 6/6/2017
# Chapter 8 - Script 2

URL="https://www.google.com/finance?cid=983582"
FN=outfile1.txt                # output file
```

```
TF=temp1.txt                    # temp file for grep


loop=1
while [ $loop -eq 1 ]
do
 rm $FN 2> /dev/null            # remove old file
 curl -o $FN $URL               # output to file
 rc=$?
 if [ $rc -ne 0 ] ; then
   echo "curl returned code: $rc"
   echo "outfile:"
   cat $FN

   exit 200
 fi

 echo ""                        # carriage return
 date
 grep "ref_983582_l" $FN > $TF
 echo -n "DJIA: "
 cat $TF | cut -c 25-33

 sleep 1h
done

exit 0
```

Here's what it looks like on my system. Normally you would probably leave the progress information out of the output by using the -s option but I thought it looked cool and so left it in:

```
guest1@big1:~/LinuxScriptingBook/chapters/chap8
File  Edit  View  Search  Terminal  Help
guest1 $ script2
  % Total    % Received % Xferd  Average Speed   Time    Time     Time  Current
                                 Dload  Upload   Total   Spent    Left  Speed
100 94006     0 94006    0      0 98740       0 --:--:-- --:--:-- --:--:--  142k

Tue Jun  6 16:55:19 HST 2017
DJIA: 21,136.23
guest1 $ 
```

You can see that curl and wget work pretty much the same way. Remember when writing scripts such as these to keep in mind that the format of the page will almost certainly change from time to time so plan accordingly.

Summary

In this chapter we showed how to use wget and curl in scripts. The default behavior of these programs were shown as were some of the many options. Return codes were also discussed and a couple of example scripts were presented.

The following chapter will cover how to more easily debug both syntax and logic errors in your scripts.

9
Debugging Scripts

This chapter shows how to debug Bash shell scripts.

Programming in any language, be it C, Java, FORTRAN, COBOL*, or Bash can be a lot of fun. However, what is often not fun is when something goes wrong, and when it takes an inordinate amount of time to find the problem and then solve it. This chapter will attempt to show the reader how to avoid some of the more common syntax and logic errors, and also how to find them when they occur.

*COBOL: Okay, I have to say that programming in COBOL was never fun!

The topics covered are in the chapter are:

- How to prevent some common syntax and logic errors.
- The shell debugging commands such as `set -x` and `set -v`.
- The other ways to set up debugging.
- How redirection can be used to debug in real time.

Syntax errors

Nothing can be so frustrating than to be on a roll when coding your script or program and then have a syntax error pop up. In some cases the solution is so easy you find and solve it right away. In other cases it can take minutes or even hours. Here are a few pointers:

When coding a loop put the whole `while...do...done` structure in first. It is sometimes really easy to forget the ending `done` statement, especially if the code spans more than a page.

Take a look at *Script 1*:

Chapter 9 - Script 1

```sh
#!/bin/sh
#
# 6/7/2017
#
echo "Chapter 9 - Script 1"

x=0
while [ $x -lt 5 ]
do
 echo "x: $x"
 let x++

y=0
while [ $y -lt 5 ]
do
 echo "y: $y"
 let y++
done

# more code here
# more code here

echo "End of script1"
exit 0
```

And here is the output:

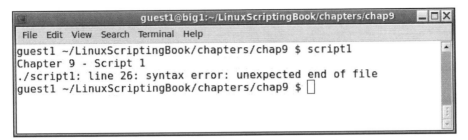

Look at this real closely, it says the error is at **line 26**. Wow, how can that be, when the file has only has 25 lines in it? The simple answer is that's just the way the Bash interpreter handles this type of situation. If you have not already found the bug it's actually at line 12. This is where the `done` statement should have been and by omitting it I intentionally caused the error. Now imagine if this had been a really long script. Depending on the circumstances it could take a long time to find the line that caused the problem.

Now take a look at *Script 2*, which is just *Script 1* with some additional `echo` statements:

Chapter 9 - Script 2

```
#!/bin/sh
#
# 6/7/2017
#
echo "Chapter 9 - Script 2"

echo "Start of x loop"
x=0
while [ $x -lt 5 ]
do
  echo "x: $x"
  let x++

echo "Start of y loop"
y=0
while [ $y -lt 5 ]
```

```
do
  echo "y: $y"
  let y++
done


# more code here
# more code here


echo "End of script2"
exit 0
```

Here is the output:

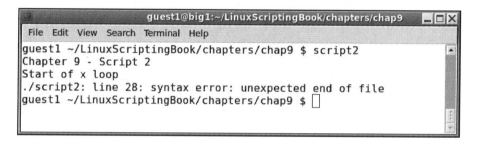

You can see that the `echo` statement `Start of x loop` was displayed. However, the second one, `Start of y loop` was not displayed. This gives you a good idea that the error is somewhere before the 2nd `echo` statement. In this case it is right before, but don't expect to be that lucky every time.

Automatic backups

Now for a bit of free programming advice, making automatic backups of files was mentioned in *Chapter 4, Creating and Calling Subroutines*. I strongly suggest you use something like this when you are writing anything that is even slightly complicated. There is nothing more frustrating than to be working on your program or script and have it going pretty well, only to make a few changes and have it fail in some bizarre fashion. You had it working a few minutes ago and then wham! It has a fault and you can't figure out what change caused it. If you don't have a numbered backup you could literally spend hours (maybe days) trying to find the bug. I have seen people spend hours backing out every change until the problem was found. Yes, I have done it too.

Obviously if you have a numbered backup you can simply go back and find the latest one that doesn't have the fault. You can then diff the two versions and probably find the error really fast. Without a numbered backup, well you are on your own. Don't do what I did and wait 2 years or more before realizing all of this.

More syntax errors

A fundamental problem with shell scripts is syntax errors don't usually show up until the line with the problem is parsed by the interpreter. Here's a common error that I still find myself doing more than I should. See if you can locate the problem by just reading the script:

Chapter 9 - Script 3

```
#!/bin/sh
#
# 6/7/2017
#
echo "Chapter 9 - Script 3"

if [ $# -ne 1 ] ; then
 echo "Usage: script3 parameter"
 exit 255
fi


parm=$1
echo "parm: $parm"

if [ "$parm" = "home" ] ; then
 echo "parm is home."
elif if [ "$parm" = "cls" ] ; then
 echo "parm is cls."
elif [ "$parm" = "end" ] ; then
 echo "parm is end."
```

```
else
  echo "Unknown parameter: $parm"
fi


echo "End of script3"
exit 0
```

Here's the output:

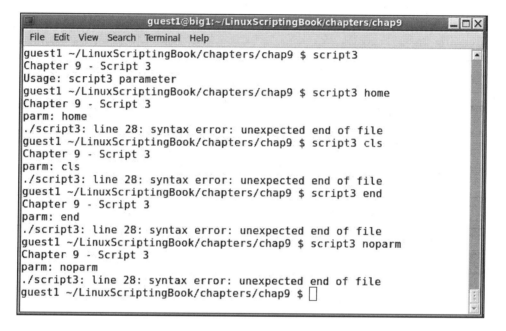

Did you find my mistake? When I code an if...elif...else statement, I tend to copy and paste the first if statement. I then prepend elif to the next statement but forget to remove the if. This gets me almost every time.

Look at how I ran this script. I started first with just the name of the script to invoke the Usage clause. You may find it interesting that the syntax error was not reported by the interpreter. That's because it never got down to that line. This can be a real problem with scripts, as it may run for days, weeks, or even years before running a part of code that has a syntax error in it and then failing. Keep this in mind when writing and testing your scripts.

Here is another quick example of a classic syntax error (classic in the sense that I just now made it again):

```
for i in *.txt
 echo "i: $i"
done
```

When run it outputs this:

```
./script-bad: line 8: syntax error near unexpected token `echo'
./script-bad: line 8: ` echo "i: $i"'
```

Can you find my mistake? If not look again. I forgot the `do` statement after the `for` statement. Bad Jim!

One of the easiest things to do wrong in a script is to forget the $ in front of a variable. This is particularly so if you code in other languages such as C or Java, because you don't prepend a $ to variables in those languages. The only real advice I can give here is if your script just doesn't seem to be doing anything right check all of your variables for the $. But be careful you don't go too far and start adding them where they don't belong!

Logic errors

Now let's talk about logic errors. These can be very hard to diagnose, and unfortunately I don't have any magical ways to avoid those. There are some things that can be pointed out however to help track them down.

A common problem with coding is what is called off by 1 errors. This was caused when computer language designers in the sixties decided to number things starting at 0 instead of 1. Computers will happily start counting anywhere you want them to and never complain at all, but most humans tend to do better when they start counting at 1. Most of my peers would probably disagree with this, but since I was the one who always had to fix their off by 1 defects I stand by my comments.

Let's look at the following very simple script:

Chapter 9 - Script 4

```
#!/bin/sh
#
# 6/7/2017
#
```

```
echo "Chapter 9 - Script 4"


x=0
while [ $x -lt 5 ]
do
 echo "x: $x"
  let x++
done


echo "x after loop: $x"
let maxx=x


y=1
while [ $y -le 5 ]
do
 echo "y: $y"
  let y++
done


echo "y after loop: $y"
let maxy=y-1                      # must subtract 1


echo "Max. number of x: $maxx"
echo "Max. number of y: $maxy"


echo "End of script4"
exit 0
```

And the output:

```
guest1@big1:~/LinuxScriptingBook/chapters/chap9
File  Edit  View  Search  Terminal  Help
guest1 ~/LinuxScriptingBook/chapters/chap9 $ script4
Chapter 9 - Script 4
x: 0
x: 1
x: 2
x: 3
x: 4
x after loop: 5
y: 1
y: 2
y: 3
y: 4
y: 5
y after loop: 6
Max. number of x: 5
Max. number of y: 5
End of script4
guest1 ~/LinuxScriptingBook/chapters/chap9 $
```

Look at the subtle differences between the two loops:

- In the x loop the counting was started at 0.

- x was incremented while it was less than 5.

- The value of x after the loop was 5.

- The var maxx, which is supposed to equal the number of iterations, is set to x.

- In the y loop the counting was started at 1.

- y was incremented while it was less than or equal to 5.

- The value of y after the loop was 6.

- The var maxy, which is supposed to equal the number of iterations, is set to y-1.

If you already understand the above perfectly you will probably never have a problem with 1 off errors and that's great.

For the rest of us I suggest looking over this very carefully until you get it just right.

Using set to debug scripts

You can use the `set` commands to help with debugging your scripts. There are two common options to `set`, x and v. Here is a description of each.

Note that a - activates the set while a + deactivates it. If that sounds backwards to you it is because it is backwards.

Use:

- `set -x`: to display the expanded trace before running the command
- `set -v`: to display the input line as it is parsed

Take a look at *Script 5* which shows what `set -x` does:

Chapter 9 - Script 5 and Script 6

```
#!/bin/sh
#
# 6/7/2017
#
set -x                          # turn debugging on

echo "Chapter 9 - Script 5"

x=0
while [ $x -lt 5 ]
do
 echo "x: $x"
 let x++
done

echo "End of script5"
exit 0
```

And the output:

```
guest1@big1:~/LinuxScriptingBook/chapters/chap9          _□X
 File  Edit  View  Search  Terminal  Help
guest1 ~/LinuxScriptingBook/chapters/chap9 $ script5
+ echo 'Chapter 9 - Script 5'
Chapter 9 - Script 5
+ x=0
+ '[' 0 -lt 5 ']'
+ echo 'x: 0'
x: 0
+ let x++
+ '[' 1 -lt 5 ']'
+ echo 'x: 1'
x: 1
+ let x++
+ '[' 2 -lt 5 ']'
+ echo 'x: 2'
x: 2
+ let x++
+ '[' 3 -lt 5 ']'
+ echo 'x: 3'
x: 3
+ let x++
+ '[' 4 -lt 5 ']'
+ echo 'x: 4'
x: 4
+ let x++
+ '[' 5 -lt 5 ']'
+ echo 'End of script5'
End of script5
+ exit 0
guest1 ~/LinuxScriptingBook/chapters/chap9 $ □
```

If this looks a little strange at first don't worry, it gets easier the more you look at it. In essence, the lines that start with a + are the expanded source code lines, and the lines without a + are the output of the script.

Look at the first two lines. It shows:

```
+ echo 'Chapter 9 - Script 5'
Chapter 9 - Script 5
```

The first line shows the expanded command and the second the output.

You can also use the `set  -v` option. Here is a screenshot of *Script 6* which is just *Script 5* but with `set  -v` this time:

```
guest1@big1:~/LinuxScriptingBook/chapters/chap9        _ □ X
File  Edit  View  Search  Terminal  Help
guest1 ~/LinuxScriptingBook/chapters/chap9 $ script6

echo "Chapter 9 - Script 6"
Chapter 9 - Script 6

x=0
while [ $x -lt 5 ]
do
  echo "x: $x"
  let x++
done
x: 0
x: 1
x: 2
x: 3
x: 4

echo "End of script6"
End of script6
exit 0
guest1 ~/LinuxScriptingBook/chapters/chap9 $ 
```

You can see the output is quite a bit different.

Note that with the `set` commands you can turn them on and off at any point you want in the script. This is so you can limit the output to just the areas of the code you are interested in.

Let's look at an example of this:

Chapter 9 - Script 7

```
#!/bin/sh
#
# 6/8/2017
#
set +x                          # turn debugging off

echo "Chapter 9 - Script 7"
```

```
x=0
for fn in *.txt
do
 echo "x: $x - fn: $fn"
 array[$x]="$fn"
 let x++
done


maxx=$x
echo "Number of files: $maxx"


set -x                      # turn debugging on


x=0
while [ $x -lt $maxx ]
do
  echo "File: ${array[$x]}"
  let x++
done


set +x                      # turn debugging off


echo "End of script7"
exit 0
```

And the output:

```
guest1@big1:~/LinuxScriptingBook/chapters/chap9                    _ □ X
File  Edit  View  Search  Terminal  Help
guest1 ~/LinuxScriptingBook/chapters/chap9 $ script7
Chapter 9 - Script 7
x: 0 - fn: bak-0001.chapter9.txt
x: 1 - fn: bak-0002.chapter9.txt
x: 2 - fn: chapter9.txt
x: 3 - fn: chapter-template.txt
Number of files: 4
+ x=0
+ '[' 0 -lt 4 ']'
+ echo 'File: bak-0001.chapter9.txt'
File: bak-0001.chapter9.txt
+ let x++
+ '[' 1 -lt 4 ']'
+ echo 'File: bak-0002.chapter9.txt'
File: bak-0002.chapter9.txt
+ let x++
+ '[' 2 -lt 4 ']'
+ echo 'File: chapter9.txt'
File: chapter9.txt
+ let x++
+ '[' 3 -lt 4 ']'
+ echo 'File: chapter-template.txt'
File: chapter-template.txt
+ let x++
+ '[' 4 -lt 4 ']'
+ set +x
End of script7
guest1 ~/LinuxScriptingBook/chapters/chap9 $ □
```

Notice how the debugging was explicitly turned off at the beginning of the script even though it is off by default. This is a good way to keep track of when it is off and when it is on. Look at the output closely and see how the debug statements don't start displaying until the second loop with the array. Then it is turned off before running the last two lines.

The output when using the set commands can be pretty hard to look at sometimes and so this is a good way to limit what you have to wade through to get to the lines of interest.

There is another debugging technique that I use quite frequently. In many cases I think it is superior to using the set commands as the display does not get quite as cluttered. You may recall in *Chapter 6, Automating Tasks with Scripts*, that we were able to display output to other terminals. This is a very handy feature.

The following script shows how to display output in another terminal. A subroutine is used for convenience:

Chapter 9 - Script 8

```sh
#!/bin/sh
#
# 6/8/2017
#
echo "Chapter 9 - Script 8"
TTY=/dev/pts/35                  # TTY of other terminal

# Subroutines
p1()                            # display to TTY
{
 rc1=0                          # default is no error
 if [ $# -ne 1 ] ; then
  rc1=2                         # missing parameter
 else
  echo "$1" > $TTY
  rc1=$?                        # set error status of echo command
 fi

 return $rc1
}

# Code
p1                              # missing parameter
echo $?

p1 Hello
echo $?

p1 "Linux Rules!"
```

```
echo $?


p1 "Programming is fun!"
echo $?


echo "End of script8"
exit 0
```

And the output:

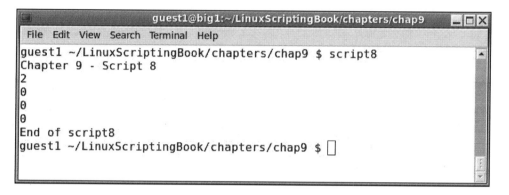

Remember to quote the parameter to `p1` in case it contains blank characters.

This subroutine might be a bit of overkill to use for debugging but it captures many of the concepts previously discussed in this book. This approach can also be used in a script to display information in multiple terminals. We will go over that in the next chapter.

 When writing to a terminal if you get a message similar to this:
`./script8: line 26: /dev/pts/99: Permission denied`

It probably means the terminal has not been opened yet. Also remember to put your terminal device strings into a variable because those tend to change after a reboot. Something like `TTY=/dev/pts/35` is a good idea.

A great time to use this debugging technique is when writing a form script as we did in *Chapter 5, Creating Interactive Scripts*. So, let's take a look at that script again and put this new subroutine to use.

Chapter 9 - Script 9

```
#!/bin/sh
# 6/8/2017
# Chapter 9 - Script 9
#
TTY=/dev/pts/35            # debug terminal


# Subroutines
cls()
{
 tput clear
}


move()                     # move cursor to row, col
{
 tput cup $1 $2
}


movestr()                  # move cursor to row, col
{
 tput cup $1 $2
 echo -n "$3"              # display string
}


checktermsize()
{
 p1 "Entering routine checktermsize."

 rc1=0                     # default is no error
 if [[ $LINES -lt $1 || $COLUMNS -lt $2 ]] ; then
  rc1=1                    # set return code
 fi
 return $rc1
}
```

```
init()                          # set up the cursor position array
{
  p1 "Entering routine init."

  srow[0]=2;   scol[0]=7        # name
  srow[1]=4;   scol[1]=12       # address 1
  srow[2]=6;   scol[2]=12       # address 2
  srow[3]=8;   scol[3]=7        # city
  srow[4]=8;   scol[4]=37       # state
  srow[5]=8;   scol[5]=52       # zip code
  srow[6]=10;  scol[6]=8        # email
}


drawscreen()                    # main screen draw routine
{
  p1 "Entering routine drawscreen."

  cls                           # clear the screen
  movestr 0 25 "Chapter 9 - Script 9"
  movestr 2 1 "Name:"
  movestr 4 1 "Address 1:"
  movestr 6 1 "Address 2:"
  movestr 8 1 "City:"
  movestr 8 30 "State:"
  movestr 8 42 "Zip code:"
  movestr 10 1 "Email:"
}

getdata()
{
  p1 "Entering routine getdata."

  x=0                           # array subscript
  rc1=0                         # loop control variable
  while [ $rc1 -eq 0 ]
  do
```

```
    row=${srow[x]}; col=${scol[x]}

    pl "row: $row  col: $col"

    move $row $col
    read array[x]
    let x++
    if [ $x -eq $sizeofarray ] ; then
      rc1=1
    fi
  done
  return 0
}


showdata()
{
  pl "Entering routine showdata."

  fn=0
  echo ""
  read -p "Enter filename, or just Enter to skip: " filename
  if [ -n "$filename" ] ; then        # if not blank
    echo "Writing to '$filename'"
    fn=1                              # a filename was given
  fi
  echo ""                      # skip 1 line
  echo "Data array contents: "
  y=0
  while [ $y -lt $sizeofarray ]
  do
    echo "$y - ${array[$y]}"
    if [ $fn -eq 1 ] ; then
      echo "$y - ${array[$y]}" >> "$filename"
    fi
    let y++
  done
```

```
   return 0
}


p1()                            # display to TTY
{
 rc1=0                          # default is no error
 if [ $# -ne 1 ] ; then
  rc1=2                         # missing parameter
 else
  echo "$1" > $TTY
  rc1=$?                        # set error status of echo command
 fi


 return $rc1
}


# Code starts here

p1 " "                          # carriage return
p1 "Starting debug of script9"

sizeofarray=7                   # number of array elements

if [ "$1" = "--help" ] ; then
 p1 "In Usage clause."

 echo "Usage: script9 --help"
 echo " This script shows how to create an interactive screen program"
 echo " and how to use another terminal for debugging."
 exit 255
fi

checktermsize 25 80
rc=$?
if [ $rc -ne 0 ] ; then
```

```
echo "Please size the terminal to 25x80 and try again."
exit 1
fi


init                            # initialize the screen array
drawscreen                      # draw the screen
getdata                         # cursor movement and data input routine
showdata                        # display the data


pl "At exit."
exit 0
```

Here is the output from the debug terminal (dev/pts/35):

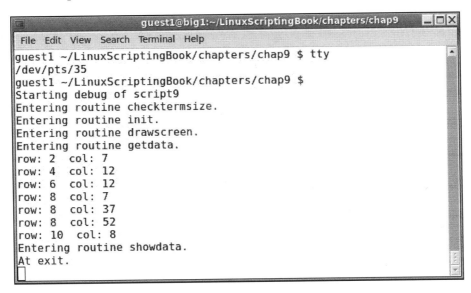

By having the debug information display in another terminal it is much easier to see what is happening in the code.

You can put the pl routine where ever you think the problem might be. Labeling which subroutine is being used can also help locate if the problem is in a subroutine or in the main code body.

When your script is completed and ready for use, you don't have to remove the calls to the pl routine unless you really want to. You can just code a return 0 at the top of the routine.

I use this approach when debugging shell scripts or C programs and it has always worked very well for me.

Summary

In this chapter we explained how to prevent some common syntax and logic errors. The shell debugging commands `set -x` and `set -v` were also described. Using redirection to send the output from a script to another terminal was also shown as a way to debug in real time.

In the next chapter we will talk about scripting best practices. This includes making careful backups of your work and selecting a good text editor. A way to help you be more productive using the command line by using environment variables and aliases will also be discussed.

10
Scripting Best Practices

This chapter explains some practices and techniques that will help the reader become a better and more efficient programmer.

In this chapter we will talk about what I consider to be scripting (or programming) best practices. Having programmed computers since 1977 I have attained quite a bit of experience in this field. I take great pleasure in teaching people about computers and hopefully my ideas will be of some benefit.

The topics covered are as follows:

- Backups will be discussed again, including verification
- I'll explain how to pick a text editor you are comfortable with and learn its capabilities
- I'll cover some basic command line items such as using a good prompt, command completion, environment variables and aliases
- I'll provide some bonus scripts

Verifying backups

I have already spoken about backups at least twice in this book and this will be the last time I promise. Create your backup scripts and make sure they run when they are supposed to. But one thing I have not talked about yet is verification of the backups. You might have 10 teraquads of backups lying around somewhere, but do they actually work? When was the last time you checked?

When using the tar command it will report at the end of the run if it encountered any issues making the archive. In general if it doesn't show anything amiss the backup is probably good. Using tar with the -t (tell) option, or actually extracting it on the local or remote machine, is also a good way to determine if the archive was made successfully.

Note: A somewhat common mistake when using tar is to include a file in the backup that is currently being updated.

Here is a rather obvious example:

```
guest1 /home # tar cvzf guest1.gz guest1/ | tee /home/guest1/temp/
mainlogs`date '+%Y%m%d'`.gz
```

The `tar` command might not consider this an error but will usually report it so be sure to check for this.

Another common backup mistake is to not copy the file to another computer or external device. If you are good at making backups but they are all on the same machine eventually the hard drive and/or controller is going to fail. You may be able to recover the data but why take the risk? Copy your files to at least one external drive and/or computer and be safe.

There is one last thing about backups I will mention. Make sure you have a backup sent to an off-site location, preferably in another city, state, continent, or planet. You really can't be too careful with your valuable data.

ssh and scp

Using `scp` to a remote computer is a really good idea too and my backup program does that every night as well. Here is how to set up unattended `ssh`/`scp`. In this case, the root account on machine 1 (M1) will be able to `scp` files to the `guest1` account on machine 2 (M2). I do it this way because I always disable root access of `ssh`/`scp` for security reasons on all my machines.

1. First make sure `ssh` has been run at least once on each machine. This will set up some needed directories and files.
2. On M1, under `root`, run the `ssh-keygen -t rsa` command. This will create the file `id_rsa.pub` in the `/root/.ssh` directory.
3. Use `scp` to copy that file to M2 to the `/tmp` directory (or some other suitable location).
4. On M2 go to the `/home/guest1/.ssh directory`.
5. If there is already an `authorized_keys` file edit it, otherwise create it.
6. Copy the line in the `/tmp/id_rsa.pub` file into the `authorized_keys` file and save it.

Test this by using `scp` to copy a file from M1 to M2. It should work without prompting for a password. If there are any problems remember that this has to be set up for each user that wants to perform unattended `ssh`/`scp`.

If you have an **Internet service provider** (**ISP**) that provides SSH with your account this method should work on there as well. I use it all the time and it is really convenient. Using this approach you can have a script generate an HTML file and then copy it right to your website. Dynamic generation of HTML pages is something programs are really good at.

Find and use a good text editor

If you only occasionally write scripts or programs then vi is probably good enough for you. However, if you get into some real in depth programming, be it in Bash, C, Java, or some other language you should very definitely check out some of the other text editors that are available on Linux. You will almost certainly become more productive.

As I mentioned before, I have been working with computers for a really long time. I started out using an editor on DOS called Edlin and it was pretty weak (but still better than punch cards). I eventually moved on and started using vi on AIX (IBM's version of UNIX). I got pretty good at using vi since we didn't have any other options yet. As time went on other choices became available and I started using the IBM Personal Editors. These were really easy to use, more efficient than vi, and had many more features. As I did more and more programming, I found that none of these editors could do everything I wanted and so I wrote my own in the C programming language. This was a long time ago under DOS, however, my editor has now been modified to run on Xenix, OS/2, AIX, Solaris, UNIX, FreeBSD, NetBSD, and of course Linux. It also works well on Windows under the Cygwin environment.

Any text editor should have the standard features such as copy, paste, move, insert, delete, split, join, find/replace, and so on. These should be easy to use and require not more than two keystrokes. The `save` command should only need one keystroke.

In addition, a good editor will also have one, more, or all of the following:

- Ability to edit more than one file at a time (file ring)
- Ability to switch to the next or previous file in the ring with a single keystroke
- Be able to show which files are in the ring and switch to any file instantly
- Ability to insert a file into the current file

- Be able to record and play back a remembered key sequence. This is sometimes referred to as a macro

- An undo/restore feature

- An auto file save option

- A locked files feature, to prevent editing the same file in another instance of the editor

- Absolutely no obvious shortcomings or bugs. This is mandatory

- Accept input via telepathy

Well, maybe I haven't quite figured out that last one yet. There are of course many, many more features that could be listed but I feel those are some of the most important.

Here's a screenshot of my editor showing an example of how the `ring` command might look:

```
┌─────────────────── guest1@big1:~/LinuxScriptingBook/chapters/chap10 ──────── _□X ┐
│ File  Edit  View  Search  Terminal  Help                                          │
│     ---- Top of file ----                                                         │
│ Chapter 1 - Getting started with shell scripting                                  │
│ Files in Ring                                                                     │
│T  1 /home/guest1/LinuxScriptingBook/chapters/chap1/chapter1.txt         NEW       │
│t  2 /home/guest1/LinuxScriptingBook/chapters/chap2/chapter2.txt         NEW       │
│   3 /home/guest1/LinuxScriptingBook/chapters/chap3/chapter3.txt         NEW       │
│T  4 /home/guest1/LinuxScriptingBook/chapters/chap4/chapter4.txt         NEW       │
│   5 /home/guest1/LinuxScriptingBook/chapters/chap5/chapter5.txt         NEW       │
│T  6 /home/guest1/LinuxScriptingBook/chapters/chap6/chapter6.txt         NEW       │
│   7 /home/guest1/LinuxScriptingBook/chapters/chap7/chapter7.txt         NEW       │
│H  8 /home/guest1/LinuxScriptingBook/chapters/chap8/chapter8.txt         NEW       │
│   9 /home/guest1/LinuxScriptingBook/chapters/chap9/chapter9.txt         NEW       │
│C                                                                                  │
│   Enter # to select: ▯                                                            │
│S                                                                                  │
│                                                                                   │
│ Show how to validate parameters by using conditional statements.                  │
│                                                                                   │
│ Explain how to determine the attributes of files.                                 │
│                                                                                   │
│                                                                                   │
│                                                                                   │
│ Here is an example of a very simple script. It might not look like much           │
│ but this is the basis for every script:                                           │
│                                                                                   │
│                                                                                   │
│ Chapter 1 - Script 1                                                              │
│ - - - - - - - - - - - - - - - - - - - - - - - - - - - - - - - - -                 │
│                                                                                   │
│ #!/bin/sh                                                                         │
│ #                                                                                 │
│ # Date                                                                            │
│ ===================================================== big1      Sat Jun 10 10:12am ===│
│ ring                                             Line   1  Col   1 NEW       340   │
│ Lewis Linux Editor 5/5/2017    chap1/chapter1.txt                                  │
└───────────────────────────────────────────────────────────────────────────────┘
```

Many more features could be shown but that should be enough to get the point across. I will mention that vi is a fine editor and is used with success by probably the majority of UNIX/Linux people. However, in my experience if a lot of programming is being done the use of a different editor with more features will save you a lot of time. It's also quite a bit easier, and that makes the process even more fun.

Environment variables and aliases

Environment variables were covered in *Chapter2, Working with Variables*. Here is a cool trick that I learned years ago that can really help when using the command line. Most Linux systems generally have several standard directories under $HOME such as Desktop, Downloads, Music, Pictures, and so on. I personally do not like typing the same things over and over again and so do this to help use the system more efficiently. Here are some of the lines that I have added to my /home/guest1/.bashrc file:

```
export BIN=$HOME/bin
alias bin="cd $BIN"

export DOWN=$HOME/Downloads
alias down="cd $DOWN"

export DESK=$HOME/Desktop
alias desk="cd $DESK"

export MUSIC=$HOME/Music
alias music="cd $MUSIC"

export PICTURES=$HOME/Pictures
alias pictures="cd $PICTURES"

export BOOKMARKS=$HOME/Bookmarks
alias bookmarks="cd $BOOKMARKS"

# Packt- Linux Scripting Bootcamp
export LB=$HOME/LinuxScriptingBook
```

```
alias lb="cd $LB"


# Source lbcur

. $LB/source.lbcur.txt
```

Using this approach you can cd to any of the above directories by just typing the lowercase alias. What's even better is you can also copy or move files to or from the directory by using the uppercase exported environment variable. Check out the following screenshot:

```
guest1@big1:~/LinuxScriptingBook/chapters/chap10            _ □ ×
File  Edit  View  Search  Terminal  Help
guest1 ~ $ down
guest1 ~/Downloads $ la
total 14412
drwxr-xr-x.  2 guest1 guest1     4096 Jun 10 15:23 .
drwx------. 46 guest1 guest1     4096 Jun 10 15:17 ..
-rw-r--r--   1 guest1 guest1  3176586 Jun 10 15:23 CaliforniaSun.mp3
-rw-r--r--   1 guest1 guest1 10505138 Jun 10 15:23 LINUX_UTILITIES_COOKBOOK.pdf
-rw-r--r--   1 guest1 guest1   293500 Jun 10 15:23 starship.jpg
-rw-rw-r--   1 guest1 guest1   768609 Jun 10 15:23 utility1.docx
guest1 ~/Downloads $ music
guest1 ~/Music $ mv $DOWN/CaliforniaSun.mp3 .
guest1 ~/Music $ pictures
guest1 ~/Pictures $ mv $DOWN/starship.jpg .
guest1 ~/Pictures $ bookmarks
guest1 ~/Bookmarks $ mv /home/guest1/Desktop/bookmarks-2017-06-10.json .
guest1 ~/Bookmarks $ lb
guest1 ~/LinuxScriptingBook $ cat source.lbcur.txt
# 4/20/2017
# Source this file from .bashrc
export LBCUR=$LB/chapters/chap10
alias lbcur="cd $LBCUR"

guest1 ~/LinuxScriptingBook $ lbcur
guest1 ~/LinuxScriptingBook/chapters/chap10 $ []
```

It took me several years to start doing this and I am still kicking myself for not discovering it sooner. Remember to make the alias lowercase and the env var uppercase and you should be good to go.

Notice the command I ran in the Bookmarks directory. I actually typed mv $DESK/ and then hit the *Tab* key. This caused the line to auto-complete and then I added the dot . character and pressed *Enter*.

Remember to use command auto-completion any time you can, it's a great time saver.

The line . `$LB/source.lbcur.txt` needs to be explained. You can see I have an `lbcur` alias which puts me into the directory where I am currently working on this book. Since I use both my root and `guest1` accounts to write a book, I can change the chapter number in just the `source.lbcur.txt` file. I then source the `.bashrc` files for root and `guest1` and I'm done. Otherwise, I would have to make the change in each `.bashrc` file. With just two files maybe it wouldn't be that bad, but suppose you had several users? I use this technique quite a bit on my systems as I am a very lazy typist.

Remember: When using aliases and environment variables you need to source the users's `.bashrc` file before any changes will be picked up in the terminal.

ssh prompt

When I run a Linux system I tend to have at least 30 terminal windows open. Some of these are logged into the other machines in my house. As of this writing I am logged into laptop1, laptop4, and gabi1 (my girlfriend's laptop running Fedora 20). I found a while back that if the prompt were different on these terminals it was harder for me to get mixed up and type the right command but on the wrong computer. Needless to say that could be a disaster. For a while I would change the prompt manually but that got old very quickly. One day I found almost by accident a really cool solution to this problem. I have used this technique on Red Hat Enterprise Linux, Fedora, and CentOS and so it should work on your system as well (with maybe a little bit of tweaking).

These lines are in the `$HOME/.bashrc` file on all my systems:

```
# Modified 1/17/2014
set | grep XAUTHORITY
rc=$?
if [ $rc -eq 0 ] ; then
  PS1="\h \w # "
else
  PS1="\h \h \h \h \w # "
fi
```

So what this does is use the set command to grep for the string XAUTHORITY. That string is only in the environment on the local machine. So when you open a terminal locally on big1 it uses the normal prompt. However, if you ssh to another system the string is not there and so it uses the long expanded prompt.

Here is a screenshot of my system showing how this looks:

Testing an archive

Here is something that I ran into on several of my computer jobs. I would be asked by my manager to take over a project from a fellow worker. He would `zip` or `tar` up the files and then give me the archive. I would uncompress it on my system and try to begin the work. But there was always a file missing. It would often take two, three, or more attempts before I would finally have every file needed to compile the project. So, the moral to this story is when making an archive to give to someone else make absolutely sure to copy it to another machine and test it there. Only then can you be reasonably sure that you have included every file.

Progress indicator

Here is another cursor movement script that also calculates the low and high of the $RANDOM Bash variable. It might not look all that cool to everyone but it does show some more of the concepts we have covered in this book. I was also somewhat curious as to what the range of that random number generator was.

Chapter 10 - Script 1

```
#!/bin/sh
#
# 6/11/2017
# Chapter 10 - Script 1
#


# Subroutines
```

```
trap catchCtrlC INT          # Initialize the trap


# Subroutines
catchCtrlC()
{
 loop=0                       # end the loop
}


cls()
{
 tput clear
}


movestr()                     # move cursor to row, col, display string
{
 tput cup $1 $2
 echo -n "$3"
}


# Code
if [ "$1" = "--help" ] ; then
 echo "Usage: script1 or script1 --help "
 echo " Shows the low and high count of the Bash RANDOM variable."
 echo " Press Ctrl-C to end."
 exit 255
fi

sym[0]='|'
sym[1]='/'
sym[2]='-'
sym[3]='\'

low=99999999
high=-1

cls
```

```
echo "Chapter 10 - Script 1"
echo "Calculating RANDOM low and high ..."
loop=1
count=0
x=0
while [ $loop -eq 1 ]
do
 r=$RANDOM
 if [ $r -lt $low ] ; then
  low=$r
 elif [ $r -gt $high ] ; then
  high=$r
 fi

# Activity indicator
 movestr 2 1 "${sym[x]}"       # row 2 col 1
 let x++
 if [ $x -gt 3 ] ; then
  x=0
 fi

 let count++
done

echo " "                       # carriage return
echo "Number of loops: $count"
echo "low: $low  high: $high"

echo "End of script1"
exit 0
```

And the output on my system:

```
guest1@big1:~/LinuxScriptingBook/chapters/chap10

File  Edit  View  Search  Terminal  Help
Chapter 10 - Script 1
Calculating RANDOM low and high ...
 |^C/
Number of loops: 185994
low: 0   high: 32767
End of script1
guest1 ~/LinuxScriptingBook/chapters/chap10 $
```

Creating new commands from a template

Since you are reading this book it can be assumed that you are going to be writing
a good number of scripts. Here is another handy trick I learned over the years.
When I need to create a new script, instead of doing it from scratch I use this
simple command:

Chapter 10 – Script 2

```sh
#!/bin/sh
#
# 1/26/2014
#
# create a command script

if [ $# -eq 0 ] ; then
  echo "Usage: mkcmd command"
  echo " Copies mkcmd.template to command and edits it with kw"
  exit 255
fi

if [ -f $1 ] ; then
   echo File already exists!
```

```
    exit 2
fi


cp $BIN/mkcmd.template $1
kw $1
exit 0
```

And here is the contents of the $BIN/mkcmd.template file:

```
#!/bin/sh
#
# Date
#
if [ $# -eq 0 ] ; then
  echo "Usage:              "
  echo "                    "
  exit 255
fi
```

Be sure that after you create the mkcmd.template file that you run chmod 755 on it. That way you do not have to remember to do it every time on your new commands. In fact, that was the main reason I wrote this script.

Feel free to modify this however you want, and of course change kw to vi or whatever editor you are using.

Alerting the user

It's nice to have your computer beep when an important task has completed and you want to know about it right away. Here's a script I use to beep the internal speaker on my computer:

Chapter 10 – Script 3

```
#!/bin/sh
#
# 5/3/2017
#
```

```
# beep the PC speaker

lsmod | grep pcspkr > /dev/null
rc=$?
if [ $rc -ne 0 ] ; then
 echo "Please modprobe pcspkr and try again."
 exit 255
fi

echo -e '\a' > /dev/console
```

This command will beep the PC speaker if it has one and if the driver has been loaded. Note that this command will probably only work on your system when run as the root user.

Summary

In this last chapter, I showed some of the programming best practices I have learned. The features of a good text editor were talked about, and a $RANDOM testing script was included. I also presented some of the scripts I have written over the years to make my systems more efficient and easier to use.

Index

validating, conditional statements
used 13, 14, 16

process
watching 48, 50

progress indicator 180, 183

R

recursion 142, 143

S

scp 174
screen
clearing 55, 56
screen manipulation 34-38
scripts
demonstrating 2-9
for checking user login 99, 100
running, as root 109-113
tasks, automating with 95-97
variables, using in 12, 13
variables, using in 11
set commands
used, to debug scripts 160-162, 164, 166, 171
shell scripting
about 1, 2
text editor, using 2
sleep command 44-46, 48, 95
ssh 174
ssh prompt 179
subroutines 58, 62
syntax errors 151-157

T

tasks
automating, with scripts 95-98
text editor
finding 175-177
using 175-177

U

Uniform Resource Locator (URL) 138
user
alerting 184

V

variables
using, in scripts 11-13

W

wget configuration files 140, 142
wget options 138, 139, 144, 145, 146
wget program 137, 142, 143, 144
wget return codes 140
who command 100

Z

zip command
used, for backing up files 106-109